RAISING GREAT KIDS

WORKBOOK FOR PARENTS OF TEENAGERS

Resources by Henry Cloud and John Townsend

Boundaries
Boundaries Workbook
Boundaries *audio*
Boundaries *video curriculum*
Boundaries in Dating
Boundaries in Dating Workbook
Boundaries in Dating *audio*
Boundaries in Marriage
Boundaries in Marriage Workbook
Boundaries in Marriage *audio*
Boundaries with Kids
Boundaries with Kids Workbook
Boundaries with Kids *audio*
Changes That Heal (Cloud)
Changes That Heal Workbook (Cloud)
Changes That Heal *audio* (Cloud)
Hiding from Love (Townsend)
The Mom Factor
The Mom Factor Workbook
The Mom Factor *audio*
Raising Great Kids
Raising Great Kids for Parents of Preschoolers *curriculum*
Raising Great Kids Workbook for Parents of Preschoolers
Raising Great Kids Workbook for Parents of School-Age Children
Raising Great Kids Workbook for Parents of Teenagers
Raising Great Kids *audio*
Safe People
Safe People Workbook
Safe People *audio*
Twelve "Christian" Beliefs That Can Drive You Crazy

RAISING GREAT KIDS

A COMPREHENSIVE GUIDE TO

Parenting with Grace and Truth

WORKBOOK FOR PARENTS OF TEENAGERS

AGES 13–19

Dr. Henry Cloud & Dr. John Townsend

with Lisa Guest

ZondervanPublishingHouse

Grand Rapids, Michigan

A Division of HarperCollinsPublishers

Raising Great Kids Workbook for Parents of Teenagers
Copyright © 2000 by Henry Cloud and John Townsend

Requests for information should be addressed to:

📖 ZondervanPublishingHouse
Grand Rapids, Michigan 49530

ISBN: 0-310-23437-9

Published in association with Yates and Greer, LLP, Literary Agent, Orange, CA

Interior design by Laura Blost

Printed in the United States of America

00 01 02 03 04 05 06 07 / ❖ DC/ 10 9 8 7 6 5 4 3 2 1

Contents

Dear Reader

Thanks for opening up this *Raising Great Kids Workbook*. We are excited about this workbook, and we hope you find it helpful in parenting your teenager.

Parenting teenagers definitely has its challenges. While the first twelve or so years of your child's life have been about parenting, the adolescent years are about de-parenting. At this point you are helping your teen prepare for the "leaving" that is soon to come. This step out of the nest involves such milestones as gaining the ability to recognize and maintain healthy relationships; relating to parents with more and more freedom—after first earning that freedom; discovering and developing gifts and talents; taking ownership of one's life; establishing self-discipline; solidifying moral and spiritual values; and beginning serious inquiry into a career path. In short, this is the period in which a child leaves childhood.

As a parent, you have been and continue to be key to your teenager's development. In fact, it is impossible to overestimate how important a role parents play in growing a child up to young adulthood. As the Bible teaches, parents are to "train a child in the way he should go" (Proverbs 22:6). But most parents feel overwhelmed by the complexity of this demanding job. With so many things to pay attention to, how does one know the real tasks and goals? Along the way, many parents become discouraged or don't even know where to start.

If you're just now beginning this process of character-based parenting, you may be concerned about "time lost." You may worry or feel guilty about not doing the right things, or doing the wrong things, in the earlier years of your teenager's life. While it is true that the earlier we help our kids' character growth the better, there are a few other points to remember.

1. Even parents who have been addressing character issues since their child's infancy make mistakes. Effective parenting is not about avoiding mistakes (that's impossible), but about knowing how to be aware of, take responsibility for, and correct what we have not done right. No child has a parent who has never made a mistake.

2. The injuries or deficiencies caused by mistakes can be repaired. With the right combination of love, truth, wisdom, and grace, a parent can both help teens recover things they may have missed in their character development and help bring healing to any damage they may have experienced. After all, God is a healer (Psalm 147:3). He is intimately and continually involved in the process of redemption.

3. Finally, you have probably done a great many "right" things that count for much in your child's character development. As you absorb the material in this workbook, you may find that you have been aligning your parenting with several of the principles we address even though you haven't had a systematic structure like this one. Kids of all ages thrive on the correct amount of grace, truth, and time. As you have applied these in the past, your child has grown.

We wrote *Raising Great Kids* to help parents, whatever their children's ages and whatever challenges they face. The book is a comprehensive resource that provides a structure for approaching parenting. It provides a road map for creating *character* in kids—and character is the ability to function as God has designed them to function in the world. The biblical principles apply to all ages and stages, so you can start using them today as a guide. We have provided lots of examples, illustrations, and suggestions to help you apply the information.

The organization of *Raising Great Kids* differs in a major way from this workbook. The book itself is not arranged by age. By design, we included no infancy, toddler, school-age, or teen sections. Instead, we organized the material by principles universal to all stages of parenting. For example, the character trait of connectedness applies to the infant who is learning to reach out for Mother's love, to the school-age child who is learning how to make friends, and to the teenager who is attempting to connect not only to her parents but also to safe people in the outside world. By organizing the material in this fashion, we hope you will be able to see what your teenager needs in order to develop these character traits and then help provide it for her. Also, this organizational approach solves the old problem of people's tendency to read only the sections of the book that apply to them.

However, we designed the workbook differently. We have written three separate ones—one dealing with infants and toddlers, one dealing with school-age kids, and this one dealing with adolescents—so that, in this case, you can apply the universal principles in parenting situations typical of teens. A workbook is just what its name says: a book that helps you work in a practical, hands-on manner to apply principles to your specific situation. If you've read either of the other workbooks, you'll notice some similarities, especially in the early chapters where we lay the foundation for this approach to parenting. This workbook, however, addresses some of the specific issues parents of adolescents face. We pray that God will use it to help your parenting be the successful and worthwhile relationship that he designed it to be.

We appreciate your labors as a parent. Happy reading, and God bless you!

HENRY CLOUD, PH.D.
JOHN TOWNSEND, PH.D.

How to Use This Workbook

The *Raising Great Kids Workbook* is designed to be used in a variety of ways.

- You will get the most out of your investment of time if you read *Raising Great Kids* as you work through this book. The text fleshes out key concepts with real-life examples and a more thorough discussion.
- You or you and your spouse—or you and a friend—can use the workbook on your own. In tandem with the text, the questions in this workbook will help you become more intentional and more effective in your parenting.
- You or you and your spouse can be part of a small group that meets regularly to discuss the challenges of parenting, share tips, and pray for each other and for your teenagers.
- Many of the key questions for parents of teens are marked with the sunglasses icon. Read all of the questions in each chapter so that you follow the logic and understand the context of any given question. But let this icon help you focus on the most crucial questions for your stage of parenting. If you are reading *Raising Great Kids* with a group, the icon may help you choose which questions to discuss.
- Whether you're tackling *Raising Great Kids* on your own, with a spouse or another parent, or in a group, be sure to include plenty of prayer time. After all, whatever the age of our kids and whatever parenting challenges we currently face, we all need God to shore up the areas in which we are lacking skills, knowledge, or energy.

May God bless you as, with his guidance, you raise a great kid.

Introduction
A Forbidden Topic

Parenting Principles

- Relationship is central not only to the order of the universe God has created, but also to parenting.
- The Bible as well as our own observation tells us that, most of all, children need love.
- Love is essential, but love alone is not enough. We must have the structure of reality and truth to make relationships and the rest of life work well.
- Parenting is a long-term job, but one day children will have to go off on their own. After they have gone, the character their parents built into them will guide them.
- Character is never complete without an understanding of who one is before God. Healthy people have the ability to see who God is, to love him, to obey him, and to take their proper role under him.

*Perhaps you've noticed for yourself that, in conversations about parenting philosophies and practices, battle lines are often drawn. Parenting is no safer a topic than politics and religion.**

- Some people advocate structure and control at the expense of everything else: to raise an obedient child is the most important thing. Others advocate love over structure: having a child feel loved and secure in love is primary. Some people emphasize the sinfulness of children while others talk about the inherent goodness and innocence of children.

---

*The parts in italics are passages from the book *Raising Great Kids*. Page references to *Raising Great Kids* are in parentheses.

— As you begin working through the *Raising Great Kids Workbook,* what do you see as a parent's primary job? Which of the four groups mentioned above (if any) comes closest to verbalizing your perspective and priorities?

— Briefly explain why you picked up this book. What do you hope to learn? What kind of help are you looking for?

• People's conversation about parenting perspectives and practices becomes impassioned because it is conversation about their children's welfare, their community, their own welfare, and their God—four aspects of their lives in which they invest their very hearts.

— What specific aspects of your teenager's welfare are you most concerned about? Many parents, for instance, worry about their adolescent's faith, friends, schoolwork, and computer time. List your four or five main concerns here. (By the way, we'll be using *adolescent* and *teen/teenager* interchangeably throughout the workbook.)

— What admonitions about parenting from people in your community do you carry around internally? When have you wanted to disagree with the advice you have received? If you bucked that advice, what happened? What risks to relationships are involved in your efforts to parent the way you believe best for your child?

— Give two or three examples of how your life is affected by how your teenager is doing. How, for instance, do your son or daughter's choice of friends, willingness (or unwillingness) to study, and decisions about sex or spirituality affect you?

— When, if ever, have you realized that a discussion of parenting styles is, in fact, a discussion of religion? How does your relationship with God impact your parenting, both theoretically and practically?

All around the country parents are discussing parenting philosophies and practices. They feel tremendous pressure to do the right thing for their child, for themselves, in light of their community, and before God. It's a daunting task. To help you in this task, we have built this book around some of the values that are most important to us. Let's look at some of these now before you go through the book.

The Value of Love (page 14)

Relationship is central not only to the order of the universe God has created, but also to parenting. You, a parent, can't construct character in your children without having a deep relationship with each one of them.

• The Bible as well as our own observation tells us that, most of all, children of all ages need love. Not only is relationship central for their development, but it is their ultimate goal in life as well. Furthermore, Jesus himself summed up the entire Jewish law in the simple statement "Love God and love others." That's why a relational system is at the core of this book.

— What experiences in your childhood taught you that you were loved— or made you feel unloved and perhaps even unlovable? Think about your teenage years in particular.

— What can you learn from your own growing-up years that will help you teach your teenagers the value of love?

Your teenagers need to be deeply related to you and others, and you are going to have to keep relationship as a goal of their development.

The Value of Truth (page 15)

Love is essential, but love alone is not enough. We must have the structure of reality and truth to make our relationships and the rest of life work well.

• Children cannot be loved too much, but they can be disciplined not enough.

— What kind of discipline (or lack of discipline) did you grow up with? What family rules were enforced during your teenage years? What were the results of the discipline you received, good and/or bad?

— Parents are dispensers of truth and reality sometimes through direct teaching, sometimes through discipline, and sometimes by getting out of the way and letting consequences do the instructing. What lessons of truth and reality did your parents teach most effectively? Which of these three methods do you remember them using—and at what point of your life?

— Again, what can you learn from your own growing-up years that will help you teach your teenager the value of truth?

Parents want each of their children to become a person of truth, living in wisdom. In the following pages, we have tried to show you what kinds of truth adolescents need and how to present it to them.

The Role of Character (page 15)

Parenting is a temporary job. One day soon your teenagers will have to go off on their own. After they have gone, the character you built into them will guide them.

- As a parent, you need to be much more concerned about what kind of "tree" (good or bad) your teenager is becoming than about any particular "fruit" you might see on a single day.

  — Is this statement challenging or freeing or, to some degree, both? Explain your answer.

  — What does the word *character* mean to you? What thoughts and questions come to mind as you consider building character into your teenagers?

In Raising Great Kids *we have always tried to see a particular parenting problem or task in light of the ultimate task of character development so that you can be more concerned about the tree rather than only the behavioral fruit of the day. We want to help you to have teens who are not only responsible now, but who become responsible adults. Anyone can obey the rules with a police officer around, but ultimately only people of character obey when no one is around to tell them what to do. So we'll define "character" and instruct you how to develop it in your teens.*

The Often-Asked Question

"Is it too late to start this character-building process when my teenager is only a few years from adulthood?" Let us reassure you that there is much you can accomplish during these adolescent years. Here's why.

1. Though they are close to being adults, adolescents are still technically children. That means that they are in a developmental process that is unfinished at this point; they are still malleable. You are working with a person who has not yet totally solidified into who she or he is to become. For that reason, you can still influence your teen in ways that encourage character growth.

2. The teenage years are years of turmoil and conflict. Adolescents feel both independent and helpless at the same time. They feel fear as well as excitement about the future. They have profoundly intense emotions and impulses, yet they are developing important values and morals. This conflicted state is a parent's ally: it provides parents with opportunities to give feedback to teenagers. Though they may not act like it, at some level teens are most likely very aware that they don't have it all together. They very much need your love, support, and truth.

3. Even if this is your first exposure to the character development model of parenting, you will probably realize that you have done a lot of things in the preteen years that are in line with this material. As you apply the principles set forth here, you will be building on the years of parenting that have helped prepare your teenager for this time of life.

4. The growth process never really ends for any of us who is submitted to God's plan (Ephesians 4:15). That means that any time of life can be very beneficial to an individual who is growing. So keep being, doing, and saying the right things, those things that will strengthen connectedness, responsibility, reality, competence, morality, and the spiritual life of your teen. You are giving your teen the same sorts of realities he or she will experience along God's path throughout life. Help your teenager to see these as normal parts of living.

An Understanding of Sin, Immaturity, and the Image of God (page 16)

We believe, first, that children are created in the image of God and have a lot of good things about them from the start. Second, children are sinners, and all of their goodness is affected by sin. Third, children do not show up already assembled: they are immature and must be "put together" by the parenting process.

- These three beliefs lead us to assert that everything an adolescent does is not necessarily bad, or good, or immature. You have to discern which is which. Furthermore, you can't judge a behavior, in and of itself, out of context of character. Consider these two examples. First, two teenagers may manifest similar defiance on a given day. One's argumentativeness over the curfew may be simply protesting and defining himself, but he knows he's going to be home by midnight. The other may be saying no to the twelve o'clock deadline because she has learned that she will get whatever she wants if she yells, whines, or cries enough.

  — Give another example or two of the kinds of behavior that might mean either neediness or manipulation. What behaviors might be the image of God manifesting itself (good assertiveness) or disobedience (sinful rebellion)?

  — What kinds of clues help you determine what is motivating your teenager's behavior at a particular moment?

It is important to give to immature teenagers who are in need and incomplete. It is important to discipline adolescents who rebel against truth, you, God, and structure. It is important to nurture the very potential God built into them.

The Value of Freedom (page 17)

God created people to grow into self-control (Galatians 5:23). So it is important for you to play a role in your teenagers' lives that will help them gain control of themselves and their own lives.

- We believe that freedom undergirds everything God has for people (Galatians 5:1) and that this freedom is to be used responsibly in the service of love.

— What kinds of freedoms did you grow up with? Give examples from different points in your childhood. What kinds of responsibility did your parents require of you at those specific points in time? Comment on the balance they maintained between freedom and responsibility. (Was it effective and reasonable? Did it help you mature or did it hinder that process?)

— In what ways, if any, did your parents prepare you for eventually taking control of your own life? (Does a certain conversation with one of them or one of their pet phrases stand out in your mind?) What can you learn from your own experience and apply to your own parenting?

We will help you to not fear the freedom of your teenagers, but at the same time to require responsibility from them.

The Role of God (page 17)

Character is never complete without an understanding of who one is before God. Healthy people have the ability to see who God is, to love him, to obey him, and to take their proper role under him.

• God gave parents the assignment of bringing up children to love and be in relationship with him and, eventually, to take their proper place in life as his children (Deuteronomy 6:20–25).

— Did your parents fulfill this God-given assignment? If so, what did they do? What can you learn from what they did right (or wrong) in this regard?

— What would you have liked to have received from your parents in the way of spiritual training and guidance? What are you doing to give your teenagers those very things?

We want to help you help your teenagers understand God and his values and their role before him. We also want to help you help them understand God's love and his ways. So this will be another thread throughout the book.

The Process (page 18)

Parenting is a process that begins with conception or adoption and ends many years later. What you need to do as a parent will change every day. But once you understand the principles involved, you will be more likely to do the right thing and enjoy raising great kids.

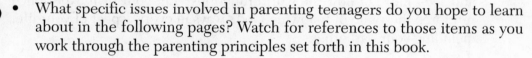

• What specific issues involved in parenting teenagers do you hope to learn about in the following pages? Watch for references to those items as you work through the parenting principles set forth in this book.

Godspeed (page 19)

Parents want to do the right thing, and they can—given the right help. We hope you will find this book to be one of many helps available to you.

• Carefully consider three of our main points:

1. Balance the role of love with the need for limits.
2. Value the worth of the kids God has given you without turning them into little gods.
3. Teens have much potential but need a lot of both nurturing and correction to achieve that.

— Which of these points do you have the easiest time acting on?

— Which one is the most challenging? Why? What might you do to improve your chances for success in that area?

- Ultimately, we believe in God's plan for parenting as outlined in the principles of the Bible. We don't, however, believe in a particular rigid way of following those principles.

    — What biblical principles come to mind that can serve as guidelines for your parenting?

    — What biblical truths have you come to appreciate more as you've grown and seen more of how the world functions? Let your own experience reinforce the value of following God's ways in every aspect of your life, including your parenting.

Pray hard, get lots of support, implement what we suggest, and enjoy the trip. And may God be with you each and every step along the way as you raise some great kids!

Hands-on Exercise

If You Do One Thing Besides Pray . . .

Before getting into the material more deeply, pause to summarize what you hope to learn and list any specific questions you have about parenting your teenager. You can refer to this page along the way to make sure you're learning what you want to learn and then, at the end, to see what God has shown you about the quite daunting but extremely rewarding call to parent.

Folded-Hands Exercise

"My help comes from the LORD . . ."

—PSALM 121:2

Lord God, the chapter's closing statement—both a charge and a benediction—reinforces what I already know: I need you in my efforts to parent the teenagers you have entrusted to me. You have blessed me in some amazing ways throughout my life, but never with a gift as precious as my kids. And I've had some tough stewardship issues along the way, but nothing like this. Parenting an adolescent definitely keeps me on my knees praying hard! Lord, give me discernment and creativity as I look for ways to help my teenager become a person of godly character. Show me where to go and on whom to lean for support. And please help me sense your guiding and empowering presence with me so that I can enjoy the trip. I'm thankful that you'll be with me every step of the way, redeeming my mistakes, guiding my efforts, and blessing my attempts to raise my teenager to live a life that pleases and glorifies you. I pray in Jesus' name. Amen.

Part One

Raising Children of Character

The Goal of Parenting

A Child with Character

Parenting Principles

- The parent's task is to develop a little person into an adult.
- The issue along the way is not about being good, but about having good character.
- Character is the sum of our abilities to deal with life as God designed us to.
- As a child grows up, parents transfer more and more freedom and responsibility from their shoulders to their child's.
- Growing character always involves the elements of development and internalizing.

Everybody wants good kids. Good children do what they're supposed to do, so this is a proper and right desire. The issue is not about merely being good, because many good children don't grow up handling life well. They may become either not-so-good people or good, but immature, adults. As my (John's) friend Tony learned, the issue is not about being good, but about having good character (pages 23–24).

The Importance of Being a Parent (page 24)

If you are a parent of an adolescent, you have been engaged in one of the most meaningful jobs in the world. You have been doing—and are continuing to do—eternally significant work: developing a little person into an adult.

- What routine and mundane aspects of the huge and relentless task of parenting often keep you from being focused on the eternal significance of your work?

- You chauffeur to school and church activities. You negotiate about clothes and curfews. You monitor grades, music, computer time, and friends. You try to choose the battles to fight, which issues to go to the wall for. With all this (and more) going on, what helps—or could help—you keep your eyes on the big picture and ultimate goal of parenting your teenager?

As a parent, you may find it hard to get your head above water long enough to figure out exactly what you're trying to accomplish and how you will know when you get there. Parents need a way to keep in mind the ultimate goal of parenting: creating an adult.

Creating an Adult (page 25)

We parents define success not by how our kids are doing today, but by what happens after they leave home.

- What hopes for your soon-to-be-adult do you have for the following aspects of his life?

— School

— Job

— Dating

— Marriage

— Friendships

— Personal values and conduct

— Spiritual life

- One of the elements of childhood is dependency, but God designed children to function independently of you one day. For many years, you have been investing in helping your child leave you, and you're almost at that point. What can you learn—or have you learned—from moms and dads you've seen experience and deal well with the pain of parent-wounds that come as their child grows up? What source(s) of strength and comfort did they draw on? If you don't know, ask them.

Sadly, kids don't always grow up well. Sometimes they don't leave, and they depend on their parents far too long. At other times they leave, but they aren't prepared for adult life. They are adults on the outside, but they are broken or undeveloped on the inside.

Who Is Responsible for What? (page 26)

Who is responsible for your teenager's maturity and readiness for the world—you or your teen? We believe in the following three principles about responsibility.

1. Responsibility lies on a continuum between child and parent, and where it lies on the continuum changes over time. Around the beginning of the teen years, the parent actively begins "de-parenting," that is, exchanging a controlling role in the child's life for an influential one. By the time he reaches the late teens, the child should be taking over more or less total responsibility for his behavior, finances, morality, and relationships.

— Have you noticed a shift in your role as parent from control to influence? If so, describe the difference. If not, what can you do to actively begin "de-parenting"? Be specific about what you will do and when you will do it.

 — What evidence do you see that your teenager is moving toward taking over total responsibility for her behavior, finances, morality, and relationships? Again, be specific.

— What do you find helpful about the idea that the amount or kind of responsibility a child has lies on a continuum? How does this image help you approach the task of parenting your teen?

2. Even though responsibility shifts, both parents and teenagers still have their own unique and distinct tasks.

— On the one hand, what are you doing to provide safety and love for your teenager (your tasks as a parent)? On the other hand, what, if anything, are you doing to ask your teen if it's okay to be a parent? (The question "Is it all right with you if I set a midnight curfew?" does not show parental authority.)

 — What can you do to help your adolescent take on greater responsibility? For example, what kind of schedule and system of rules for doing chores and homework—and consequences for not doing them—could you establish? What rules and consequences regarding curfew and grades would be appropriate and effective? Where, if at all, do you need to stop rescuing your teenager from the consequences of his actions? Are you, for instance, making excuses for late homework assignments? Are you giving too many second chances for violations of curfew?

 — The child's tasks are to take risks, fail, and learn lessons. What greater risks have you seen your teenager take since entering junior high school or high school? How have you—or how do you want to—respond to your teen's risk taking and failures?

3. Children must bear the ultimate responsibility for their lives.

— What can a parent do to help an adolescent learn this truth? What will you do, for instance, to stay emotionally connected to your teen while keeping good limits with her? Instead of retracting the consequence, what will you say, for example, when your angry teenager has lost driving privileges because she didn't observe the established curfew?

— What happened during your adolescence, if anything, that helped you learn that you are ultimately responsible for your life?

As teenagers come more and more to terms with what are their tasks and what are not, they always need to be moving toward full responsibility for their lives and souls.

Your Parenting Reflects Your Goals (page 27)

Ironically, we often know our financial and career goals more clearly than we do our parenting goals.

- As a parent, you have many fires to put out, and today's worries keep you busy enough. But take a moment here and indicate which of the following goals your parenting reflects.

Survival	Independence/self-sufficiency
Competence	Problem solving
Morality	Religious life

- Now consider the list again as well as any other possibilities. What goal(s) would you like your parenting to reflect? What changes might you have to make for that to happen?

My friend Tony wanted his daughter Halley to be a good kid. Good kids are a product of the real goal of parenting: mature character. When children grow up with mature character, they are able to take their place as adults in the world and function properly in all areas of life. Character growth is the main goal of parenting.

Character: The Real Goal (page 29)

But what is character?

- Who among your friends and acquaintances would you describe as a person of good character? List two or three people.

- For some, *character* means having integrity, being responsible, and standing for the right thing. We would agree that these are desirable qualities. However, we view character as the structures and abilities within ourselves that make up how we operate in life. In other words, character is *the sum of our abilities to deal with life as God designed us to*.

— Consider the people of character you listed above in light of this broader definition. What "abilities to deal with life" do their lives reflect?

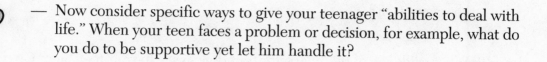

— Now consider specific ways to give your teenager "abilities to deal with life." When your teen faces a problem or decision, for example, what do you do to be supportive yet let him handle it?

- You may know adults who look good and perform well, but who have character flaws (a bad temper, a tendency to withdraw, or self-centeredness) that diminish their life experience. More often than not, these flaws began in childhood and continued on in life.

  — Which of your own character flaws have their roots in your childhood? Explain.

  — What lessons in character do you wish you had learned when you were young?

  — What might you do to teach your teenager the lessons you missed? Be specific.

When you help your teenager develop character, you are addressing the heart of parenting. Character provides a tool kit of spiritual and emotional skills that prepare a teen to succeed in life.

The Aspects of Character (page 31)

What does character look like? In part 2 we will explain in detail the six distinct aspects of character, but we'll start thinking about each aspect now by answering the three questions that appear with the list below.

- *Attachment:* the ability to form relationships

    (1) What did your parents do right (or wrong) to help you develop this character trait?

    (2) What evidence of this character trait do you see in your teenager? Give specific evidence of growth and/or of the need to grow in this area.

    (3) What is one thing you might do now to help your teenager further develop this aspect of character?

- *Responsibility:* taking ownership of one's life and seeing it as one's own problem

    (1) What did your parents do right (or wrong) to help you develop this character trait?

    (2) What evidence of this character trait do you see in your teenager? Give specific evidence of growth and/or of the need to grow in this area.

    (3) What is one thing you might do now to help your teenager further develop this aspect of character?

- *Reality:* the ability to accept the negatives of the real world

    (1) What did your parents do right (or wrong) to help you develop this character trait?

    (2) What evidence of this character trait do you see in your teenager? Give specific evidence of growth and/or of the need to grow in this area.

(3) What is one thing you might do now to help your teenager further develop this aspect of character?

- **Competence:** the development of everyday life skills as well as their God-given gifts and talents

  (1) What did your parents do right (or wrong) to help you develop this character trait?

  (2) What evidence of this character trait do you see in your teenager? Give specific evidence of growth and/or of the need to grow in this area.

  (3) What is one thing you might do now to help your teenager further develop this aspect of character?

- **Conscience:** an internal sense of right and wrong

  (1) What did your parents do right (or wrong) to help you develop this character trait?

  (2) What evidence of this character trait do you see in your teenager? Give specific evidence of growth and/or of the need to grow in this area.

  (3) What is one thing you might do now to help your teenager further develop this aspect of character?

- **Worship:** learning that God loves them and is in charge of life; learning to seek God on their own

  (1) What did your parents do right (or wrong) to help you develop this character trait?

  (2) What evidence of this character trait do you see in your teenager? Give specific evidence of growth and/or of the need to grow in this area.

(3) What is one thing you might do now to help your teenager further develop this aspect of character?

It is important to note here that these character aspects are attributes of God's own character. The difference is that while God has always had these character traits, an adolescent is in the process of developing them. Your first, last, and best goal is to be a good agent of developing mature character within your teenager's life and soul.

How Character Is Developed (page 32)

Growing character always involves two elements: development, *training through experience and practice; and* internalizing, *taking those experiences inside to become a part of one's personality.*

- Teaching transfers information from one person to another. But teaching alone doesn't make an adolescent "own," or take responsibility for, that information. We learn and grow from what we engage in. You can't learn how to ride a bicycle from just reading a book: you have to get on a bike. What is one lesson you learned "the hard way" (by experience) as you were growing up?

- In teaching or developing character, you will provide a wealth of experiences to help your kids engage in and learn about realities such as relationship, responsibility, forgiveness.

  — What has your teenager learned about relationships during these often tumultuous adolescent years? What, for instance, has the first broken heart taught about attachment (the ability to form relationships), reality (accepting the negatives of the real world), trust, and so on?

  — What realities have the consequences of his behavior taught your teenager? What did losing his starting position on the football team due to poor grades teach your teen about responsibility—or what lessons could have been learned if you hadn't stepped in to help? Give two or three examples from your own life.

While it's important to teach kids about loving and being loved and about taking responsibility (Deuteronomy 6:20–25), information is never enough. Teenagers need many experiences in which they see reality and adapt to it—or suffer the consequences of ignoring it.

How to Know What to Develop (page 35)

Character development is a complex assignment. You must deal with several character aspects at once; you don't have the option of working on one issue until it is resolved and then moving to the next. Kids need to be growing in each area continuously, but with different tasks appropriate to their level of maturity as they grow.

- Adolescents struggle with overconfidence in their abilities yet their constant failure in relating to their parents and the opposite sex. What experiences could help your teenager deal with that struggle?

- What areas of competence is your teenager currently working on mastering?

- What are you doing to encourage your teenager's spiritual growth? What evidence of growth, if any, do you see? Be specific.

This book provides a road map you can use to further evaluate how your teenager is doing in the major character areas—connectedness, responsibility, reality, competence, morality, and worship/spiritual life.

Fruits and Roots (page 36)

When you understand and interact with your teenager on a character level, you will quickly find that what seems to be a problem isn't really the problem. After all, you can't see or touch character. What you can see is how your teen responds to life.

- An adolescent's behavior, attitudes, and emotions serve as indicator lights about character issues.

 — What character issues might sulking, dressing provocatively, swearing, spending hours on the Internet, or choosing friends you don't approve of point to? A lack of attachment? An inability to sense responsibility for the consequences of one's actions? Something else?

 — What could you do to address the real issues behind such behaviors? What limits could be set and what consequences enforced? Then what could be done to eliminate that behavior?

- Effective parents look for what a symptom reveals about their teenager's struggle to grow up. These parents then help their teen deal with the root problem.

Now that you have the big-picture goal of parenting as character building, the next two chapters will explain the ingredients God has provided that help parents produce growth toward character in their kids: grace, truth, and time.

Hands-on Exercise

If You Do One Thing Besides Pray . . .

Make a point of regularly talking to your teen about his or her day. Asking questions that can be answered with yes or no don't count as much as questions that invite more information (although you still run the risk of getting a one-word answer). Try asking what happened in biology class, see how your teen coped with the difficult math teacher today, or follow up on something that's going on in a friendship. Then, if your teenager shares and you are able to put his experience into your own words, he will feel that you empathically "get" what he is saying. Attachment—a key element of character—will be happening.

Folded-Hands Exercise

"My help comes from the LORD . . ."

—PSALM 121:2

Thank you, Lord, for entrusting my kids to my care. What a gift each one is—and what an awesome responsibility! I thank you that you love my teenagers even more than I do and that you are there for me as I continue this task and privilege of parenting. Please, God, guide me as I try to develop in my teenager the character traits of attachment, responsibility, reality, competence, morality, and a spiritual life that glorifies you—and then, Lord, please protect and grow those traits to full fruition! I pray in Jesus' name. Amen.

Two

The Ingredients of Grace and Truth

Parenting Principles

- Parents need to show their teenagers grace, to show that they are for them.
- Parents need to give their teenagers truth, to give them reality and necessary limits.
- Grace helps teenagers tolerate dealing with truth.

Did Dan and Karen's conversation sound familiar (pages 38–39)? Do you and your spouse frequently find yourselves on different sides of the argument when you need to decide between "cutting some slack" or enforcing the limits? Or, even more common, do you find yourself at odds with yourself on this issue?

Grace and Truth Divided (page 39)

The ingredients we need as we parent our teens toward character growth—grace and truth—are separate and different elements. Choosing between the two is not the problem. Getting them together is. An effective parent must learn to be gracious and truthful at the same time.

Consider the two ingredients:

1. Your teenagers need to know that you are on their side. You do this by showing them empathy. This expression of grace, or favor, is an environment that allows growth. As grace is taught and modeled, as you let your teens know that "I am for you," grace is experienced and internalized by your teens.

2. Your teens need to know that you will give them reality and set necessary limits, and that is truth. Truth is in accord with God's standards, the timeless realities he wove into his creation. Truth is the state of being reliable and trustworthy.

- Turn to pages 40–41 and look again at the lists of forms and qualities in which grace and truth manifest themselves.

    — Which group do you practice more easily than the others? Why do you think that comes more easily?

    — What do you think keeps you from offering the other to your teenager? What might you do to overcome or remove these barriers?

- Grace and truth need to come together in our parenting. During an adolescent's angry outburst, for instance, you need to stay emotionally connected to her even though she is behaving badly. At the same time, you need to hold to the truth, to the standard that the behavior is in fact unacceptable.

    Case Study #1: A teen who has made good grades in school is suddenly getting Cs and Ds. One parent feels that being supportive and understanding will help. The other parent simply wants to take away privileges until the grades get better and doesn't even try to figure out why the grades may be dropping (developmental issues, drugs, depression, defiance, testing limits, etc.). How would you bring grace and truth together in this situation?

Case Study #2: A teenager gets caught drinking. Again, one parent hopes that love and faith will make the problem go away. The other wants to take away all of the teen's privileges. What would you do to balance grace and truth?

Case Study #3: An adolescent's argumentativeness got intense and even hurtful. One parent says it's part of being a teenager and let it go. The other parent demanded an instant attitude adjustment. Again, what might be an effective balance of grace and truth?

 — As you've parented adolescents, when have you noticed that you are struggling to get grace and truth together? You may, for instance, find yourself becoming angry when your teenager repeatedly ignores your instruction to get enough sleep at night rather than allowing consequences, not your anger, to train her.

 — In one of the situations you just identified, what could you have done to be gracious and truthful at the same time?

 — Now describe a situation or two in your home where grace and truth have indeed come together for you.

Bringing grace and truth together is an ongoing challenge for parents. In fact, depending on how you were raised, you may be struggling to get them together for yourself. (Remember the possible paths Dan and Karen's son Jason

could take?) Most of us can identify with some aspect of feeling divided between grace and truth.

Integration (page 42)

One goal of parenting is to integrate grace and truth. From the earliest days on through adolescence, parents must at the same time love their kids and provide limits and structures. They must be loving and firm. They must be kind but require their children to do their part. They must be compassionate and forgiving but require the children to change and be responsible.

- A rule of thumb for integrating grace and truth is "Be soft on the person but hard on the issue."

  — As you were growing up, when (if ever) were your parents soft on you but hard on the issue? Give details about the situation and about your response to their parenting in that moment.

  — Consider a typical parenting situation (enforcing a curfew that's earlier than her friends' curfew, responding to the use of inappropriate language, dealing with suggestive dress, addressing your teen's lack of desire to go to church, etc.). In the situation you select, what words to your teen would be soft on the person but hard on the issue? Be specific.

- As you try to live out the rule of thumb "Be soft on the person but hard on the issue," remember that grace establishes and maintains the quality of the relationship, and truth adds direction for the growth and structure of an adolescent's behavior and performance.

  — Earlier you identified which is easier for you to offer your teen: grace or truth. Look again (page 43 in the text) at how Dan and Karen each added the missing ingredient to their parenting. Below list two or three statements appropriate for a parenting situation you frequently face. Be sure that they reflect the addition of either grace or truth to your parenting.

Example: Your fourteen-year-old did not budget her allowance and now wants you to give her money so she can go to the movies with her friends. "Honey, I know you'd really like to see the movie on the day it's released, but we've talked about budgeting your money. I can't give you a loan. Maybe next time you'll save more and have some money when you need it."

Situation #1:

Situation #2:

Situation #3:

— Consider now your adolescent's perspective. What is helpful about this balance between grace and truth? Why does this balance improve your relationship as well as your teenager's behavior?

• As your kids grow up, your expression of grace and truth needs to change. At different ages they need different kinds of kindness and structure. But the formula is the same: grace and truth must go together.

— Turn to the chart on pages 43–47 and read the Adolescence and College Age sections. What, if anything, surprises you about what you found in the Grace category? in the Truth category?

— Review the statements listed in the columns of Grace and Truth. What tips for parenting your teen do you find there?

The grace + truth formula is the same for toddlers and collegians. Both grace and truth need to be in the mix. Few parents would subscribe to just one of those ingredients (just one of the columns in the chart), but many parents end up operating out of primarily one column. For kids to develop character, they need to be given grace and truth in virtually every interaction with their parents.

Why These Two? (page 47)

In parenting literature throughout the ages, grace and truth stand out. Mostly, one hears them referred to as love and limits. Why? Because back in the beginning God created human beings in his own image.

- Again and again the Bible describes God as a God of grace and truth, of compassion and truth, of mercy and righteousness.

  — When have you experienced God's grace, compassion, or mercy in a very personal way? Be specific. Was his grace completely divorced from his truth in those circumstances? Explain.

  — When have you experienced God's truth and righteousness in a very personal way? Again, be specific. Did God's truth seem completely divorced from his grace in that situation? Explain.

  — King David prayed, "Do not withhold your mercy from me, O LORD; may your love and your truth always protect me" (Psalm 40:11). What kind of protection does love offer? What kind of protection does truth offer?

- As God lives out his grace and truth, we are to live them out as well. We need to have the love that sustains our relationships and the truth that guides us to safety and good performance—but we are not born with these qualities fully developed. Good parents help kids grow and expand their capacities for grace and truth. The model of grace and truth that good parents offer their children helps the children internalize grace and truth.

  — What, if anything, about your parents' modeling helped you both experience and internalize grace and truth? What can you learn about parenting from what your parents taught you by their modeling, good or bad?

  — Remember Kelly's "Stupid girl!" when she dropped the doll (page 49)? That response was quite different from the four-year-old who exclaimed, "Oops! That's okay" as she went to get some paper towels to clean up the Coke she had just spilled. Think about a time when your teenager made a mistake, said something "stupid," or blew an exam at school. What did his or her response suggest about the kind of voice that has been internalized? Is it one of truth without grace or one of grace? Also, consider for a moment what you are modeling.

- The maxim is this: "What was once outside becomes inside." Give kids grace and give them truth. But don't give one without the other. Adolescents will not be able to put grace and truth together if they have not experienced them together. Let your teenagers discover that reality—truth—is actually *for* them and not *against* them.

  — When was the first time you realized for yourself that reality (or truth) is actually for you? Describe the situation, what prompted your insight, and your reaction to it.

— What can you do to help your teenagers see that reality or truth is for them, not against them? You might teach your fifteen-year-old, for instance, that if he brings his science and English grades up from a C to a B, you'll treat him to a new CD of his choice. You might teach your seventeen-year-old that if she does her chores, she will be able to go out with her friends on Friday night. Give one or two other possible scenarios from your own home.

Grace shows your teenagers favor, that someone is for them and on their team. It helps them tolerate dealing with the truth. Truth shows them that reality is real and how to live it. Give your kids both—as well as the important ingredient we'll look at in the next chapter.

Hands-on Exercise

If You Do One Thing Besides Pray...

We express grace when we show empathy; we express truth when we explain what limits are necessary in a given situation. List three recent conflicts with your teenager.

1.

2.

3.

Grace: For each, note what your teenager might have been feeling (tired, frustrated, angry, discouraged, and so on). With what words could you acknowledge such feelings?

Truth: What limits do you need to set in each situation you described? With what words could you clearly set and stick by those limits?

Folded-Hands Exercise

"My help comes from the LORD ..."

—PSALM 121:2

Father God, I can't give to my teenager what I don't have myself. Please show me which way I tend to err—toward grace or truth—and then, Spirit, work in my heart to teach me and transform me. Help me integrate grace and truth where I haven't, so that I can give to my kids a taste of the parent love—with its perfect balance of grace and truth—that you give me. I pray in Jesus' name. Amen.

——— Three ———

The Ingredient of Time

┌─ **Parenting Principles** ──────────────────────┐

- Along with grace and truth, time is the third necessary element of growth.
- Time allows the process of character growth to occur continuously.
- Grace + Truth over Time = Growth

└──────────────────────────────────────┘

Parents can learn a lot from Kayo Dottley. That football coach gave his players the grace of his encouragement and the truth of his knowledge and correction, and he mixed those with the needed time to build the skills and character they would need for later success. Let's take a look at some of the ways the ingredient of time works in the development of character.

The Nature and Importance of Time (page 51)

In this chapter we want to look at time and its relation to a person's development. We will consider the time you need to put in, how you structure that time, and the amounts and kinds of time the teen needs.

- Look back at your own childhood and the time you spent with your parents.

  — How much time did your mother and/or father invest in raising you? How much time did they spend with you during your teenage years? Refer to three or four scenes to support your sense that it was a lot of time or a little or something in between.

— How, if at all, did your parents structure time with you when you were a teenager?

— Did the time your parents gave you meet your needs, especially during your adolescent years? Explain your answer.

• Now consider the time you are spending with each of your kids.

 — How much time in a typical day and a typical week are you intentionally investing in your teenagers? "Intentionally investing" means focusing on your teen's growth. It might mean, for instance, going for a bike ride, working together on a homework assignment, collaborating on a household project, or planning the week's menus.

 — Describe the structure you give your time with your teenager.

— Are you giving enough time to meet your teen's needs? On what are you basing your answer?

Let's look at how the three aspects of time listed above—the time you need to put in, how you structure that time, and the amounts and kinds of time a kid needs—relate to your teenager.

More Time, Please (page 52)

"Quality time" versus "quantity time" is a false choice society often presents parents. Quantity of time is important because growth is happening—continuously—and you must be there throughout the process.

- Quantity of time is also important because your teens are internalizing things from the outside world, so you have to be constantly monitoring what they internalize. The analogy here is filling a car's tank with gas. A teenager takes in love and structure and converts them into character. Just as an engine can't suck down all twenty gallons at once and get you to the destination instantly, you can't feed love and structure into your teen all at once. You need to distribute the fuel as your teenager needs it.

— What about the car engine analogy do you find helpful?

— Teachers, coaches, extracurricular activities, friends, parties, the Internet—a lot of different people and things in their ever-widening world can influence the thoughts and behaviors of adolescents. Which influences do you need to monitor for your teen? What additional influences do you expect to encounter at some point in the future?

— Consider your teen's journey toward adulthood. What kind of regular fuel stops do you want to schedule (or at least be ready for) between now and then? At what points might there be an intense need for refueling, for pouring love and structure into your teenager? Transition periods such as starting high school, taking final exams, applying for college, and breaking up with a boyfriend or girlfriend are some possibilities.

- Quantity of time is important because teenagers need to grow in relationship with another person in order to develop character. We can only truly mature in relationship with other people, because relationship provides safety, love, encouragement, truth, and reality. For some people, various aspects of their personalities have been developed outside of relationship and have never been accepted or affirmed by another person. These aspects (assertiveness, pain, or sexuality, for instance) remain hidden in a dark corner of the soul.

  — Imagine a teenager who, as a little girl, grew up with parents who withdrew every time she asserted herself. While other aspects of the child (such as her love and compliance) were in relationship, her parents' withdrawal meant that her separateness was in isolation. This seventeen-year-old may now be unable to set limits because there was no love to nurture her assertiveness, or she may be able to set limits, but based on her early experience, she feels alone and guilty when she does. What aspect(s) of your personality were not accepted or affirmed by another person as you were growing up?

  — Look again at Debbie's story (pages 54–55 in the text). What, if anything, does it show you about yourself? What does it show you about the kind of parenting you do or do not want to do?

  — Your teenager needs to experience all of the aspects of himself with you. Over time, he needs to bring the various aspects of himself into relational experience with you. Which of the following aspects might you be uncomfortable embracing, and why? What can you do to overcome that hesitation rather than communicate it to your teen?

Needs	Failure
Weakness	Talents
Vulnerability	Opinions
Hurt	Assertiveness

Sadness   Honesty
Anger   Sexuality
Strength

When you spend time with all aspects of your teenagers, they are able to integrate all of those aspects of themselves into relationship and not have hidden, split-off parts to their character. Those experiences take quantities of time, but make sure that you are not just passing time and that instead you are relating to all the different aspects of your teen.

The Way the Process Works (page 55)

Teaching and internalizing character requires a certain kind of experience of time, not just "knowledge." Internalizing a new skill, habit, or moral teaching is a process—one that involves ignorance, failure, and disobedience on the part of the teen and discipline, encouragement, and teaching on the part of the parent.

- Review the five steps in the process of teaching and internalizing character outlined on pages 56–57 of the text and highlighted below.

  1. Introduce adolescents to the reality. Don't expect them to know what you expect.
  2. Allow adolescents to experience the limits of their abilities. They will fail when they try something new. If they are learning a new rule, they may not obey it the first time. A parent must set a limit by saying that to disobey a rule is "not okay" if inherent rebellion is behind the "failure."
  3. Transform the failure. When failure and discipline hurt, empathize with and contain your teenager's feelings. Empathy paves the way for teens to identify with the limit or reality of their performance. In contrast, anger, guilt, and shame distance them from the reality they need to internalize.
  4. Help your teenagers identify with the reality. If they feel understood and loved while they see the reality of their actions (#3), they will take in the reality of the rule. It becomes part of them.
  5. Encourage your teenager to try again. When learning new skills, teens have to try and fail and then try again.

• Now apply this five-step process to two current parenting issues with your teenager (getting to school on time; staying on top of schoolwork; being respectful toward adults; keeping her room neat; etc.). At which step do you find yourself in each situation? What is your next move?

Situation #1   **Situation #2**
1.   1.

2.   2.

3.   3.

4.   4.

5.   5.

• Character development requires experience. You cannot tell children—even teenagers—how to do something and instantly expect them to do it correctly. Instead, you must walk them through the process, help them when they fail, and aid them in making normal failure (such as making mistakes when learning to drive, not scoring the goal that would have won the soccer game, experiencing the end of a dating relationship, not being accepted to college) a learning experience that becomes part of their character.

— What did you learn about failure as you were growing up?

— What might you do to help your teenager make normal failure a learning experience?

The learning steps outlined above are a specific sequence of events in time. This is why parenting takes time and cannot be done from a distance. An adolescent needs time to go through the experience, and a parent needs time to discipline and to empathize with the teen's failure. Then the experience becomes character.

The Time the Child Needs (page 58)

Most parents realize that they have to spend time with their kids. Let's look at why time is important for teens.

• Time is important for kids because they can't accomplish certain tasks before they're developmentally ready.

— In what area of life or toward what behavioral goal might you be pushing your teenager too hard?

— Review the normal timeline for a child's development (pages 59–60) and some of the tasks at different stages of development (pages 61–62), focusing especially on where a teenager typically is. What did you learn about your teen?

— What, if anything, did you see about where to stop pushing your teenager?

 — In what areas of life, if any, could you be encouraging your teenager to move ahead?

- Kids cannot accomplish something "before its time." There are critical windows of time for certain developmental tasks. The general thinking is that children need to go through these stages at the appropriate time because windows open up at a certain time in their development. This may be more obvious for younger children, but requiring totally mature emotions, attitudes, and values from teenagers disrupts the more important task they are working on at that age. During adolescence, independence is at a whole new level. Sexuality is budding. Dating and opposite-sex relationships enter the scene. Adolescents question their morals, values, and ethics. The peer group becomes a powerful influence, and parents need not only to provide guidelines, but also to begin letting go.

  — In what ways is our culture rushing your teenager to grow up? What can you do to stand strong against that pervasive pressure?

  — What kind of pressure is your teenager feeling from peers? Look for positive influences as well as negative.

— In what ways are you beginning to let go of your teenager? Be specific.

As Solomon said, "There is a time for everything, and a season for every activity under heaven" (Ecclesiastes 3:1). So don't rush your teen; enjoy the process of growing up and maturing.

Remember All Three (page 63)

We have talked about the time you must put in, the way this time gets structured, and the time a teenager needs. We feel strongly that time is a necessary ingredient for character growth.

• Time, however, must be integrated with the other two important ingredients we've addressed—grace and truth. Here's the formula:

Grace + Truth over Time = Growth

— Why is giving grace and truth from time to time insufficient?

— Why is giving only truth over time prison?

— Why is giving only grace over time disastrous?

Your teenagers need to know that you are on their side, and that is grace. They need to know that you will give them reality, and that is truth. And they need it pretty much every day. Take a deep breath—and have a good time!

Now that you know the three ingredients you need to raise a great kid, we'll describe how you can go about using these three ingredients in developing the six character traits every adolescent needs to become a mature adult.

Hands-on Exercise

If You Do One Thing Besides Pray . . .

What plan do you have or will you make for regularly spending time with your teenager? This can be a tricky assignment if it means new behavior for both of you, so start slowly. When can you catch a movie or wash the car together? (Initially, a shared activity may be easier than face-to-face, one-on-one time.) Or when could you grab a Coke or go out to dinner together? Is every other Saturday a good starting point for investing time in your teenager and fueling his or her tank with love and limits?

Folded-Hands Exercise

"My help comes from the LORD . . ."

—PSALM 121:2

Father God, you've given me many gifts—your Son, forgiveness, the hope of eternal life with you, a family, a home, financial resources, food, clothes. You've also given the gift of time. Lord, I confess poor stewardship in that area and my tendency to let the sin of busyness rather than godly priorities guide my use of time. Lord, you have given me charge over my kids. Teach me to live so that my daily planner reflects my commitment to them. Help me stand strong against the culture that says quality time is adequate. May I spend quantity time with them that is also quality time in which I point my teenager to you. I pray in Jesus' name and for his—and my teenager's—sake. Amen.

Part Two

Developing the Six Character Traits
Every Child Needs

—— Four ——

Laying the Foundation of Life
Connectedness

┌───┐
Parenting Principles ──

- Connectedness is the capacity to relate to God and others on a deeply personal level.
- Connectedness is foundational to all growth and morality.
- The development of connectedness in children requires specific tasks on the part of both parent and child.
└───┘

Remember Chris? He was comfortable in his own world, which had lots of good things in it but no people. And he wasn't lonely. He was simply not able to experience a need for relationships.

Life Equals Relationship (page 68)

Because Chris was unable to make attachments, he was separated from life itself. He didn't experience a need for connection, but he was suffering from this lack of connection.

- Connectedness or, more technically, attachment (the words are interchangeable) may seem oddly categorized as a "character trait." But connectedness is foundational to all morality and is the most important trait you'll address in this book. It is the capacity to relate to God and others, to connect to something outside of ourselves. When we make an attachment, good things—such as empathy, comfort, truth, and encouragement—are transferred between us and others. Connectedness brings warmth, meaning, and purpose to life.

— What evidence have you seen that, from the womb, children are designed to connect?

— Why is attachment "foundational to all morality"?

Connectedness is not humanity's idea, but God's. God himself is relational at his core: He is love (1 John 4:8). In some fashion that we don't fully understand, the Father, Son, and Spirit are attached and related to each other at all times. The persons of the Trinity are always in relationship with one another.

The Importance of Attachment (page 69)

We cannot overemphasize the importance of developing your teenager's ability to attach. All of the tasks of life are based, at some level, on how connected we are to God and others. You cannot lose by developing your teen's ability to relate, because the attached person is never left without a way to get the resources necessary for life.

- Life brings many demands, problems, and requirements. Connected teenagers look within themselves for what they can provide and then go to God and others for the rest. Detached teens fend for themselves, unable to reach out for resources and help.

  — Would you describe yourself as a connected or a detached teenager? Support your answer with specific details.

  — What contributed to your being connected or detached? Learn from what your parents did or didn't do. Did they, for instance, comfort you when you were sad or afraid, or were they distant when you needed reassurance?

- Why does it make sense that teenagers who are emotionally connected in healthy ways are more secure and better able to delay gratification, respond to discipline, deal with failure, and make good moral decisions? (The list does go on and on.)

  — Remember Dylan and Spencer (page 70 of the text)? Dylan was an "outie." You always knew where he was emotionally. Good, bad, or green, he was clear as to how he felt about life. Spencer was an "innie." No amount of coaxing would get him out of his shell. Now think about your adolescent in the same way. Is she an "outie" or an "innie"? Give specific evidence in support of your answer. What parenting challenges does this kind of personality create—and what are you doing to meet those challenges?

Dylan and Spencer took very different approaches to a similar problem. Dylan knew he couldn't deal with the problem himself, so he went to his parents and received comfort, support, and structure so that together they could solve the problem. Spencer, however, wasn't able to reach out to family and friends to meet life's demands.

Infancy: The Birthplace of Attachment (0–12 Months) (page 71)

- Research supports the biblical idea that relationship is crucial to life. Severe disruption of the attachment between mother and child in the early months of life can affect the child's entire life. In your own words, explain the deep spiritual implications of early attachment between mother and child.

A child who is allowed to emotionally depend on reliable, loving parents becomes fortified with the assurance of their stability. As children internalize their mother's love, they feel safe enough to confidently explore the world.

Attachment Goals for Your Child (page 72)

The ability to connect can be broken down into different categories, and the foundational "inviting to life" work is done in the first year. But helping your teenager with bonding experiences continues through adolescence.

- **Use Relationship for Equilibrium:** Good attachment stabilizes adolescents. Just as God quiets his people with his love (Zephaniah 3:17), you can quiet your teenager's turmoil with your attachment.

 — Do you think your teen finds you interested in his life? safe enough? predictable enough? On what do you base your answer?

 — What are you doing to continue being bonded to your teenager?

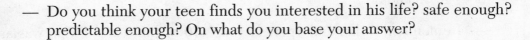 — What way(s) of showing your love does your teenager respond to most enthusiastically?

- **Learn Basic Trust and Need:** Basic trust is your teenager's ability to see the world of relationships as having enough goodness for her. You can help foster basic trust by being a "good-enough" parent—that is, being responsive at the right times and in the right ways without being perfect, just a lot more good than bad.

  — Is your basic trust (as defined above) solid and unshakable? If so, why? If not, why not? Learn from your answers a lesson to apply to your parenting.

 — You can strengthen your teenagers' basic trust by drawing out insecurities and fears of closeness, addressing those, giving rewards when risks are taken, and challenging them to trust themselves and other "safe" people. What might this look like in your home? What specific fear might you address—and how would you do that? What risk taking in the realm of relationships can you affirm? In what situation can you encourage your teens to trust themselves? And what "safe" people can you encourage your teenagers to trust?

 — Describe what a "good-enough" parent would do in one or two frequent parenting situations you may face: your teen sleeps through the alarm clock again and is late to school, realizes in the morning that the homework he thought he'd finished wasn't finished, begs to do something because "everyone else is," uses drugs or alcohol, and so on.

- **Value Relationships:** One aspect of maturity is being able to value and appreciate others' love and sacrifice for us. This creates important traits like a heart of gratitude for others and the ability to seek out and connect to people who treat them right.

  — Parents can help adolescents become people-oriented persons by talking to them and listening to them. In general, on a scale of 1 to 10 (1 being "totally preoccupied with something else" and 10 being "totally focused on your teenager"), how well do you listen to your teen? What does your answer show you about yourself?

  — Now consider how you talk to your teenager. Is it interactive? Are you listening as well as talking? Is your teenager both talking and listening?

— What are you (or could you be) doing to teach or remind your teenager that her actions affect you and sometimes even hurt you?

 — What are you doing to teach and require heartfelt gratitude?

- ***Internalize Love:*** A teenager's many experiences of safety and consistency combine over time into a stable internal mental and emotional representation of you. Ultimately, a teen doesn't think, "Mom loves me, so I'm okay," but "I'm a loved person, and I'm okay."

 — Are you being there for your teenager—for the fun stuff (celebrating the highs as they come; attending after-school activities whether they're sports events, musical presentations, school plays, or the like) as well as the necessary "life" stuff (supporting schoolwork, helping with college and career decisions, offering some financial support for extracurricular activities, etc.)—in quantity as well as quality? Point to specific examples.

 — Providing many occasions when you are there for your teenager's needs helps her internalize love. What are you doing, however, to gradually induce her to draw upon that internal love rather than you all the time? Give specific examples, such as trusting her to follow the family's rules for using the Internet, counting on her to establish a study schedule that works for her, and letting her be responsible for her own morning devotions.

- ***Develop Capacity for Loss:*** Success in life involves learning to deal with loss. An attached adolescent learns to protest, mourn, and resolve loss by bringing loss to relationship and eventually letting go. Adolescents who don't attach may devalue what they lose, stay stuck in a protest mode, or chronically mourn.

— How does your teenager typically deal with loss?

— With what kinds of words do you sympathize with your teenagers' losses (the fact that they don't get what they want; for instance, your thirteen-year-old isn't getting a CD player until his grades are up, and your seventeen-year-old won't be allowed to stay out all night after the prom)? (Don't change your mind and alter the limits so that your teenager can avoid sadness! The lesson this teaches isn't helpful!)

• ***Mature in Their Gender Roles:*** Learning to relate as male and female becomes a primary focus of adolescence. This involves consolidating one's sexual identity, dealing with emerging sexual feelings and behaviors, and learning how to secure healthy relationships with the opposite sex.

— Consider how comfortable your adolescent is being male or female. What, if anything, concerns you about how your teen is living out his or her sexuality at this point? Is behavior appropriate? Is communication about sexuality and guy-girl relationships open and comfortable?

— What evidence of healthy interaction with the opposite sex do you see in your teen's life? Is there a serious boyfriend or girlfriend? Does your teen do a lot of things with mixed groups? What lessons, if any, have relationships with the opposite sex offered your teenager?

- ***Relate to the World:*** Adolescents use relationship as a springboard of safety from which to explore the world. Attachment also helps them sort through what they like and don't like.

  — What aspects of the world is your teenager currently exploring? What are you doing to encourage that exploration?

  — What is your teen liking and not liking these days? What are you doing to further develop her interests in sports, art, music, or a specific skill? What might you do to broaden her horizons?

- ***Develop Give-and-Take:*** Another aspect of growing up is learning that relationships require give-and-take.

  — What evidence do you see that your teenager realizes that other people don't exist for her sake and that they have their own needs? Be specific.

  — What (if any) bad or selfish attitudes in your teenager are you inadvertently rewarding? What are you doing—or what could you be doing—to encourage your teenager to show interest in other family members and friends? What consequences does she suffer when she doesn't show interest in others?

  — What are you modeling about give-and-take in the relationships your teenager witnesses you in?

- **Teach Altruism:** The most mature attachment skill is selfless giving. Altruism is giving out of concern for another without regard to oneself. It is the essence of God's love.

    — Growing up is a pretty self-centered endeavor, and adolescence is a pretty self-centered season. But kids can nevertheless learn all through life that they can comfort with the comfort that they themselves have received (2 Corinthians 1:3–4). What opportunities to encourage altruism in your teenager do you find in your family? in church settings? elsewhere?

    — What selfless love (*not* martyr love, but a love based on free and good-natured choice) are you offering or modeling for your teenager? Consider your expressions of empathy or gratitude. When, if ever, have you been able to reward your teen for showing compassion for friends?

Again, while the foundational "inviting to life" work is done in the first year, helping teenagers with bonding experiences continues through their adolescence.

How Attachment Happens (page 77)

Specific tasks create the ability to connect. Kids have their job: they must experience the reality that relationship is good and that it brings the necessary elements of life. Parents have their job: they invite their kids into relationship by responding to them and meeting their needs. These two jobs interact to help kids become capable of making attachments to people.

- Think back on your own childhood and how this dance played itself out.

    — In the home in which you grew up, did you experience the reality that relationship is good, that it brings the necessary elements of life? If not, when and from whom did you learn those essential lessons? If you still need to learn these lessons, what might you do to reach that goal? Our books *Changes That Heal* (Henry Cloud, Zondervan, 1992) and *Hiding from Love* (John Townsend, Zondervan, 1996) can help.

— What did your parents do to invite you into relationship? In what ways did they respond to you? In what manner did they meet your needs?

Let's now look more closely at the tasks involved for both the teens and the parents.

- **The Teen's Tasks:**

— *Experience, and respond to, the need for relationship.* How does your teenager express his relational needs (comfort, encouragement, love, affection)? How does your teenager express functional needs (help with homework, input about college/career options)?

— *Keep signaling the need.* What evidence do you see that your teenager will keep signaling or calling until help comes?

— *Receive the good.* What evidence have you seen that your teenager doesn't receive the good passively, but instead goes out to find it and then actively responds to love?

As teenagers perform the three tasks just outlined, they receive the fuel of existence and experience the goodness of relationship, so that they continue to seek relationships.

• **The Parent's Tasks:**

— *Respond to the need.* What support do you have as you tackle the demands of parenting a teenager?

— *Adolescents need predictability.* What structure and consistency have you built—or could you gradually build—into your teenager's world?

— Discipline, delay of gratification, and patience are elements of structure parents add to a teen's reality. How well does your teenager do with delay of gratification? With patience? Support your answer with a recent incident from the parenting trenches.

— *Respond appropriately.* Are you requiring your teenager to own her need and ask for help, or do you too quickly respond to a statement ("My boyfriend dumped me") and help your daughter (offering to talk to him or his parents) before she has even asked? Give a recent example.

— *Present relational solutions to relational needs.* Whether your teenager needs connection for her isolation, hurt, or loneliness or needs answers, suggestions, advice, and problem solving for her functional needs, what do you do (could you do) to teach her that relationship comes before anything? By what words and actions do you try to show understanding, warmth, and empathy? How do you show your teenager that you are listening to her? Do you, for example, let her finish her sentence before you respond? Do you help draw out her feelings? Do you stay connected to her when she protests? Do you make sure you understand your child's emotions before you address or try to contain them?

— When has simply connecting solved what appeared to be a functional problem? This happens occasionally.

— Giving three steps to solving a relationship problem when your teenager wants you just to listen is an example of an attempt to solve relational problems functionally. Evaluate your tendency to solve relational problems functionally. Is that tendency a problem for you? If so, under what circumstances are you most likely to do so?

— *Connect without intrusiveness.* Why is this task especially challenging for parents of adolescents? When have you seen your teenager suddenly move on from needing closeness to needing freedom? What is a wise way for you to move from your teenager's need for closeness to your teenager's need for freedom?

— Do you experience relationship as controlling or enmeshing and close-ness as something that will destroy, violate, or imprison you? If so, think back on how your parents may have been intrusive when you were a teenager. What can you learn from your own experience and apply to your parenting?

— The Bible says that genuine love is not self-seeking (1 Corinthians 13:5). Why is this truth good for you to remember, especially when it comes to connecting to your teen without being intrusive?

Parent your teenagers to experience connectedness and to be able to safely receive and give love. Teaching them this kind of connectedness helps build in-side them a connected foundation that will sustain them for life. This connected foundation is also the necessary building block for the aspect of character we'll be discussing in the next chapter: learning responsibility.

Hands-on Exercise

If You Do One Thing Besides Pray . . .

Often we can think we're communicating love to someone, but what we're doing or saying may not feel like love to the recipient. What words or actions most clearly communicate love to your teenager? If you're not sure, become a student of your teen. Do gifts, time, hugs, words, notes, or something else make your teenager feel most loved? If you know what makes your teen feel loved, consider how often you speak that language of love to him or her—and start making it a habit if it isn't already.

Folded-Hands Exercise

"My help comes from the LORD . . ."

—PSALM 121:2

Almighty God, it's very easy to feel overwhelmed by this task of parenting. I thank you that my help does come from you. Please help me, Lord, to know how to use relationship with my teenagers for their growth and equilibrium. Guide me as I try to teach them to trust that relationship is good; to value relationships; to acknowledge loss and to grieve appropriately; to live out healthy gender roles; to relate to the world; to practice give-and-take in relationships; and to be altruistic. Give me wisdom as I tackle these parenting tasks. Teach me to respond to my teenagers' needs—and to respond appropriately; to present relational solutions to relational needs; and to connect without being intrusive.

May I lean on you day by day, moment by moment, trusting you to make me a "good-enough" parent. And use me in my teenagers' life so that they will be able to attach to you, their heavenly Father. I pray in Jesus' name. Amen.

Five

Developing Self-Control
Responsibility

- Responsibility is the capacity to own one's life as one's problem.
- Self-control and learning limits are necessary for responsibly choosing the good and refusing the bad.
- The four qualities involved in teaching kids responsibility are love, truth, freedom, and reality.

*T*he task of parenting is to transform the child's stance from "My life is my parents' problem" to "Yikes, my life is my problem! Though my parents love me, they aren't going to clean up all the messes I make in life." And this is the second great aspect of character: the capacity to take responsibility for one's life.

Responsibility Puts Love into Action (page 87)

Caring parents want their children to do well in life. "Doing well" has to do with the functional aspects of living, how one performs. The key to "doing well" is responsibility.

- We define responsibility as *the capacity to own one's life as one's problem.* Your job as a parent is to help structure your adolescent's time and energy into activities that develop responsibility.

  — How well did you learn to be responsible as you were growing up? More specifically, what evidence of your responsibility (or irresponsibility) can you point to in your life?

— How were those lessons about responsibility (positive or negative) taught to you? Give an example or two, ideally from your teenage years. Were you, for instance, consistently rewarded for good behavior and consistently disciplined for bad?

• The idea of earning the freedom to make good moral choices is important, because some current teachings say that all you have to do is tell kids to choose good things and refuse bad things, or simply inform them of the dangers of the bad. Choices and information are indeed important to a teenager's decision making, but teens also need to practice self-control, delay of gratification, and setting and receiving limits before they can responsibly choose the good and refuse the bad.

— Think back over your life. When have you chosen the bad because you didn't practice self-control, couldn't delay gratification, or didn't set limits or acknowledge the limits that were set for you?

— When has the practice of self-control, the delay of gratification, or the setting or honoring of limits enabled you to choose the good?

— Again, it is your job to help structure your teenager's time and energy into activities that develop responsibility. What can you do to give your teen some practice in self-control? delaying gratification? honoring limits you set? For instance, rather than pleading, threatening, or nagging about grades or a messy room, what limits could you set and what consequences could you establish to encourage good effort and minimum health and safety standards, respectively?

- What can you do to be sure your teenager is earning the freedom to make good moral choices?

- The primary function of responsibility is to put love into action, to develop love by performing good works that God foreordained for us (Ephesians 2:10). *Relationship is the reason for existence. Responsibility is the means to bring about and protect relationship.*

  — What role does responsibility have in keeping alive your love for your spouse or a close friend?

- Attachment and responsibility were designed to grow together in your child in the same way that love and truth are to be integrated in your parenting. Have you ever met any nice but irresponsible adolescents? In each case, who was paying for their lack of control or ownership of their life?

Love and limits must go together. When they do, the fruit is great. If you have any doubt, look again at page 89 and the list of abilities that comes with learning to be responsible.

Develop Responsibility With or Without Your Child's Permission (page 90)

Having teenagers who take responsibility for their life is a good and appropriate goal for parents. Yet there is one fundamental problem: from the beginning, an adolescent has no interest whatsoever in becoming responsible.

- Children (even adolescents) can't see value in taking responsibility for a problem.

  — What evidence of this truth, if any, have you seen in your teenager either recently or in the past?

— What are you teaching your teenagers if you often take on responsibilities for them that they should be bearing for themselves? When, for instance, have you noticed that, once you stopped requiring your teenager to set the table for dinner, he began expecting you to, having concluded that it is no longer his job, but yours?

— What lessons about responsibility, and what truths or untruths about yourself and your abilities, did you learn from the way your parents did or didn't take on that which was your responsibility?

• **Boundaries: Bringing Responsibility to Your Child's Experience:** Setting boundaries for your teenagers is a central part of developing responsible character in them. Boundaries are a person's property line. They point out where you end and others begin. They allow you to know what belongs to you and what belongs to another. They allow you to know what you are and are not responsible for.

 — Parents appropriately structure their children's lives so that they are free to make choices that will either reward them for responsibility or cause them pain for irresponsibility. As they grow, children experience and internalize these boundaries for themselves. What boundaries for your teenagers have you set through the years—or could you set now—that reward them for responsibility? Could you, for example, extend the curfew by a half hour on a special occasion because he has been regularly keeping the established curfew?

— What boundaries have you set—or could you set—for your teenagers that cause them pain for irresponsibility? Next time could you enforce the curfew with the consequence of making it earlier or having your teen stay home for the entire evening?

- **The Parent's Task: Love, Truth, Freedom, and Reality:** As the interaction between Kevin and Allison illustrated, your teens are not your ally in your efforts to teach them responsibility. In their minds, they have much to lose and nothing to gain by taking responsibility for their lives. But the good news is that they are going to resist responsibility whether you handle it rightly or wrongly.

  — Comment on Allison's change from frustrated psycho-mom to the calm parent who enforced logical consequences for Kevin's failure to take responsibility for his toys. What do you like about her second approach?

  — To what situation(s) with your adolescent can you apply lessons you learned from this scene with Allison?

- The responsibility you need to teach your kids can be broken down into four qualities: love, truth, freedom, and reality. As you provide these qualities in the right sequences, types, and amounts, you set up a structure for your teenagers that makes irresponsibility painful and responsibility pleasurable. And they grow as responsibility becomes internalized and part of their character structure.

  — **Love:** What do you do (or could you do) to show your teenagers that, even when you and they disagree, you are "for" them—their welfare, safety, best interests, and growth? How, for example, do you reassure them of your love during the conflict rather than withdrawing emotionally? What do you say to stay focused on the issue or behavior instead of verbally attacking your teen when you disagree?

— Did your parents' love give you the freedom to protest the rules of the household as you were learning to abide by those rules? Give an example. Did your parents' love free you from self-judgment when you failed? Again, give an example. Does your love allow your adolescent to protest house rules? To avoid self-judgment when he fails?

Continue to invest time and energy in cementing your love for your teenagers and offering them clear statements of grace. Keep in mind, too, that kids tend to shoot the messenger carrying the responsibility lesson. It hurts to have your teenager hate you, but that is part of the burden of being a parent. So stay connected and keep holding the line with your teen.

— **Truth:** It's hard to hold someone accountable for misbehaving when that person hasn't been told the truth. What do you do to make sure your teenagers understand the boundaries you are setting for them?

— Look again at the Truth column of the table in chapter 2 of the text. Review the Adolescence and College Age sections (pages 45–47). In light of what you read there, what chores can become your teen's responsibility, if they aren't already? Is your high-schooler cooking meals on a regular basis?

— Consider how you present truths to your teen. What few universal rules might replace many specific rules? What truths are you currently praying about, asking God to guide you as you determine how to present them to your teen? What trusted people can you turn to for counsel about how to present truths? Also, pages 97–98 of the text offer some ideas for effectively conveying rules. Which one(s) will you try?

— ***Freedom:*** Freedom allows adolescents to choose and then to experience the consequences of those choices. When you were growing up, did you have the freedom to disobey? What did that freedom (or its absence) teach you? How did freedom foster the growth of responsibility or lack of freedom inhibit it? Were you given consequences when you exercised freedom in bad ways?

— Think about your interactions with your teenager. Could he be living in fear of loss of love, abandonment, attack, or condemnation if he rejects your rules? Explain why you answered as you did.

— Did that green-bean situation (page 100) bring back memories? Although issues with adolescents are very different from issues with toddlers, ask yourself what parenting moments remind you that you can't control your teenager. Choose two or three of those situations and, away from the heat of the moment, develop right reasons (logical consequences) for getting your teen to do what you want him to do. Grounding and the loss of privileges can be right reasons for your adolescent to behave.

— ***Reality:*** Parenting needs to mirror the real world as much as possible, and in the real world adults experience painful consequences for their irresponsibility. When have consequences taught you an important lesson about responsibility? Ideally, refer to an experience from your teenage years.

— Review the list of qualities that make consequences effective (pages 101–2), and then look at consequences you've established through the lens those qualities provide. Are the consequences you've used—

As close to natural consequences as possible?
Appropriate to the child's developmental maturity level?
Appropriately severe?
Administered ASAP?
Loving?
As specific as possible?
Flexible?

— Keeping in mind these seven characteristics of effective consequences, establish some consequences for common infractions in your home. And remember that crossing boundaries is a kid's job. Your job is to be on the other side of the crossing and to make it unpleasant for him when he does. That way he begins to internalize the truth that being irresponsible hurts and that being responsible brings benefits.

These four responsibility builders—love, truth, freedom, and reality—all work together to create a learning and internalizing environment for adolescents. Generally, as parents remain consistent with these four, teenagers will protest, test, and escalate for a while. But when they see that you are serious and that you are stronger than they, they will develop the limits for themselves.

The Fruits of Responsibility (page 102)

Whatever their age, you can expect, observe, and encourage some things in your kids as character develops, as they begin "getting it."

- **Ownership:** Adolescents look less to Mom and Dad and more to themselves to take care of their problems.

  — What signs have you seen in your teenager that he is taking ownership of his behavior, attitudes, emotions, and relationships?

  — What are you modeling in the way of stewardship over one's behavior, attitudes, emotions, and relationships?

- **Self-Control:** As teenagers experience consistent, appropriate consequences, they take in the structure.

  — What evidence, if any, have you seen that a structure of appropriate consequences helps your teenagers finish their chores, get to school on time, be honest, or balance school and extracurricular activities? Holding off the fun stuff until chores are done, putting a clock in the bathroom, and having them miss out on special activities can be effective steps.

  — When have you caught (or later heard about) your teenager doing a good thing when you weren't looking over her shoulder and coaching her? What did you tell her in response to learning that news?

- *Freedom:* As teenagers develop self-control, they create the space in their heads to think maturely about their choices. Self-control helps them take stock of what they should and shouldn't do.

  — When has your teenager seemed to stop and consider a choice he was about to make? Be specific.

  — What did your teen's choice reveal about him and, specifically, about his progress toward being a responsible adult?

While you are training your teenagers in responsibility, don't wait for them to rise up and call you blessed. But do be encouraged by those moments when you see them developing ownership and self-control and then using that self-control to freely make good, value-based decisions.

The Motive Issue (page 104)

Parents want their teenagers to grow up to be responsible and faithful because they care and want to do the right thing, not because they're afraid of the consequences of doing the wrong thing.

- Motives are developmental: children start life as lawless and self-centered individuals and probably develop more "pure" motives to do right as they grow older. Altruism and love of God are the highest motives, but none of us is mature enough to only be driven by these.

  — What encouragement do you find in these truths about motives?

— Describe a time early on when you did the right thing because you knew it was right rather than because you feared the consequences. How old were you? What conversation went on in your head?

— What helps you today to choose to do the good and right, to love God, or to serve others? What does your own experience suggest about how you as a parent can address the motive issue with your teenager?

Accept the fact that you and your teenager are alike: you both love and care, but you both have a wayward part that needs to know about reality. (For a more complete treatment of the issue of responsibility and self-control, see our book Boundaries with Kids. *It is designed to help parents help their children take ownership over their lives, attitudes, and behaviors.)*

Attachment and responsibility form so much of a person's character. Next we will deal with how to help adolescents solve a problem as old as humankind: dealing with the reality of imperfection.

Hands-on Exercise

If You Do One Thing Besides Pray . . .

The next time you need to reinforce the importance of following rules, think about a tangible fence or boundary. Talk to your teenager about the fenced-in playground at the local elementary school. Ask him questions to get him thinking about how easy and safe it is to play ball since the fence surrounds the play area: Why is the fence there? Where do you think the kids play because of the fence? What would be different about their playing if the playground weren't fenced in? Help your teenager come to the conclusion that fences (boundaries or rules) mean safety and protection—as do your rules for him.

Folded-Hands Exercise

"My help comes from the LORD . . ."

—PSALM 121:2

Lord God, what an encouragement to realize that self-control is a fruit of your Holy Spirit's work in our lives! And what a call to pray for my teenagers—and for myself as I do my part to prepare the way for the Spirit to do his work in their hearts. And, Lord, I do pray for myself that you would give me strength to persist when my teens don't like their training in responsibility; creativity and insight as I establish boundaries and the courage to enforce them; and wisdom and guidance as I try to balance love, truth, freedom, and reality in my efforts to raise my teens to be responsible adults. May I rely on you with each step I take on this important path! In Jesus' name. Amen.

Living in an Imperfect World
Reality

— **Parenting Principles** —

- Losing well is one of the most important character traits parents can develop in their children.
- Kids need help dealing with imperfection in themselves, other people, and the world.
- Being loved should become more central than being good enough.

We don't like to lose. But in reality, we all do. And what ultimately separates the winners from the losers is not that winners lose less. It is that they lose better. And losing well, with the ability to continue on, is one of the most important character traits you can develop in your teenager.

The Lost Ideal (page 107)

Reality is a place where things do not always go as we would like. When we fail, or circumstances or relationships do not turn out as we had hoped, we have to keep going and try to make the best of a bad situation. Your teenagers' ability to do this will determine how well their lives go.

- What do you like about how you handle loss? What would you like to be able to do better when loss comes your way?

- Review the list of some ways kids experience "lost ideals" on page 107 of the text. Which of the behaviors listed have you seen in your teenager?

As a friend of mine says to her son, "Livin's hard." Your job as a parent is to make the hard job of living no more difficult than it has to be. You can do this by building into your teenager character that is able to overcome the pain and loss that everyone encounters.

The Real Loss (page 108)

In the real world, the one where we all have to live, we have a conflict between how things should be (as they were in the Garden of Eden: everything was "good") and how they really are (in our less-than-perfect world of sin and loss). As Jesus said, "In the world you have tribulation" (John 16:33 NASB).

- What losses have you experienced in your life?

- What is the earliest experience of loss you remember? What can you recall from this situation that can help you empathize with and parent your adolescent?

Learning to accept both the good and the bad enables your teenagers to have a firm grounding in reality and to create a life that will help them pursue what's left of Eden, without giving up along the way.

The Three Realities (page 108)

In this world of tribulation, kids—from the beginning of their lives—are going to have to learn to overcome imperfection in three spheres: self, other people, and the world.

- **Self:** The first reality teens have to face is this: *They are not perfect.* Adolescents often have an acutely painful awareness of their flaws, though they may try to mask it. Matt, however, never learned to accept his own imperfection. In Matt's family there is no such thing as failure, so he and his brothers never learned that they are flawed, imperfect people who will at times fail, lose, and make mistakes.

  — How did your parents respond to your failures, especially when you were in high school? Were their reactions helpful? Why or why not? How, if at all, did your parents teach you that you are not perfect?

  — How do you react to your failures? How easily do you accept the fact that you are flawed and imperfect, that you (like everyone else on this planet) will fail, lose, and make mistakes? What are you modeling to your teenager?

  — What experiences have your teenagers had that show they are flawed, imperfect people who will fail, lose, and make mistakes? Give an example or two. What did you do to help them handle the situation? What would you like to do differently next time?

  Your teenagers need to know that they are not perfect.

- **Other People:** Your teenagers also need to realize that other people are not perfect. They want others to gratify them, to never make mistakes, and certainly never to hurt them. In reality, though, they will find a whole gamut of people out there. Some are generally good and fair; others are not. Are your teens prepared for the variety of people they will meet? Are they able to tolerate other people's mistakes?

— What have you said (and what would you like to say) to your teenagers about the fact that other people are not perfect?

— What can parents do to counter the risk of raising a "brat" (someone who demands that everyone be just what she wants them to be) or a "codependent" (someone who tolerates destructive behavior from everyone)?

Learning to live with imperfect others is an important character trait.

• **The World:** Not only will your teenagers frustrate themselves and be frustrated by others, but the world will frustrate them as well.

 — What frustrations has the world introduced in your teenager's life—loss of a girlfriend or boyfriend, academic failure, a behavior problem, or something else?

— What did you do or say to help your teenager cope with that loss?

Your job is to help your teenagers develop the character that will enable them to be joyful in a world that daily gives them opportunity to be miserable. This chapter will teach you how to develop in your teens the character necessary to overcome losses, failure, sin, and evil—in themselves, in others, and in the world around them.

The Problem Defined (page 111)

In short, the problem is this: God created your kids to live in a perfect world, with perfect others, and to be perfect themselves. But now, in a fallen world, they have to live with both the ideals and the imperfections.

- What can parents do and say to help their teenagers learn to accept their imperfect self and imperfect others? Maybe you can learn something from how your parents taught you—or didn't teach you!

- How can parents force their teenagers to deal with reality yet continue to pursue their ideals? Again, what can you learn from your parents or other parents you've seen in action?

Only the internalized character of grace and truth can help teenagers negotiate life's ups and downs. And that character can only come from many experiences with a loving but truthful parent who forces them to deal with reality, accept themselves and others, and continue on to pursue their ideals.

Fig Leaves for Everyone (page 112)

When something goes wrong in life, whether inside or outside of us, we tend to make sure that neither we nor anyone else knows the truth. We have many names for this strategy, and they all fulfill the purpose of keeping the pain or badness out of our own or someone else's awareness. These strategies are aptly symbolized by Adam and Eve's fig leaves.

- When have you relied on fig leaves? Give one example.

- When have you seen your teen reach for a fig leaf in order to keep pain or badness out of her or someone else's awareness?

We adults have ways of hiding from reality just as our teenagers do. Let's look at how the fig leaves operate in the parenting process and what you should avoid. You should be aware of four barriers to building the character your teen is going to need later in life: denial of the bad things, denial of the ideals, judgment of the bad, and lack of experience of the bad things in life.

- **Denial of the Bad:** Subtle denial of their adolescents' problems or faults is very common in many couples' day-to-day parenting. Kids readily deny their own sin and problems as well.

  — We tend to have an easier time seeing other people's flaws rather than our own. When have you seen a parent deny that her teenager has a problem with, for instance, being honest or trustworthy, respecting adults, or choosing friends? Why is denial an easy path to take?

  — What problems that your teenager faces may you be unwilling to see? Are you in a close enough and safe enough relationship with another family so that other parents might help you see what you aren't letting yourself see?

  — When has your teenager readily denied her own sin, mistake, or problem? Why isn't this a good pattern for life?

- **Denial of the Ideals:** The other way to deal with the tension of living both in the good and bad is to deny the ideal altogether. This can be done in a variety of harmful ways: by labeling a teenager "the black sheep of the family," using a tone of voice that says "all bad," not being involved enough with your teen, and not pushing your teenager to perform in reasonable ways. Parents should not deny the good in either the teenager or the standard.

— Through the years, you have probably learned to see your behavior as a problem to be dealt with rather than seeing yourself as all bad when you fail. Closely related to this is the question "How has the process of failure and correction helped you accept that you are not perfect, that you are neither all good nor all bad?" What lessons from your own experience of failing and being corrected can you apply to your parenting?

— Expectations shape and form character. Dealing with our failure to meet expectations is part of the process that integrates us. Problems come when you do not expect (and then correct for) failure, when your expectations are unrealistic, or when you do not correct with grace and forgiveness. What academic and performance expectations do you have for your teenagers? Are they realistic? How do you deal with—or how would you like to deal with—their failure to meet those expectations? Practice making statements that offer grace and forgiveness.

— What pattern of being involved with your teens have you established— or would you like to establish? Point to specific evidence. Why does such involvement help them resolve the "good me–bad me" split?

- *Judgment of the Bad:* Judgment is the condemning emotional tone with which imperfection is met. In parenting we usually see judgment as anger or as crippling guilt messages about failure, and such judgment will keep a teenager from facing reality.

  — What judgment, if any, did you encounter as you were growing up, especially during your teenage years? What reality did it keep you from facing? What lesson for your own parenting can you learn from your experience?

— What might indicate that certain teenagers are afraid that their imperfections will cost them love or incur anger? What could a parent have done to sow seeds of such fear? What practical parenting tips do you find in the commands of Ephesians 4:32?

- **Lack of Experience:** Another barrier to facing reality is a lack of experience in failure.

  — When, if ever, have you seen parents *not* give their child an opportunity to fail? Why might they be afraid to let their child fail?

— Through the years, what opportunities to fail have you been able to give your now-teenage child? What lesson do you think your teenager has been learning from those experiences? What lesson(s) about failure have you wanted your teen to learn?

— What appropriate opportunity to take a risk or what freedom to attempt new skills can you offer your teenager?

Denial of the bad things, denial of the ideals, judgment of the bad, and lack of experience of the bad things in life are four barriers to building character. These barriers keep kids from learning from their mistakes, recognizing they're not as good as they think they are, realizing that failure doesn't cost them love, acknowledging that they do not know everything or know how to do everything, and becoming whole by integrating the "good me–bad me" split inside.

The Myth of "Positive Self-Esteem" (page 116)

There is a lot of talk today about self-esteem. Parents are careful to build it in their kids. People seek it for themselves. Therapists encourage it in their clients. But the whole idea of "self-esteem" is confusing for several reasons.

- First, the idea of self-esteem places the security of kids at risk by basing it on their positive performance. The concept hinges on kids being able to see themselves positively. Second, with self-esteem the focus is on maintaining a good view of ourselves as opposed to maintaining relationship. Happy people don't get all caught up in themselves; they focus more on tasks and loving other people. Third, the "good self" is a proud self, and a proud self does not develop the kind of humility before God and others that results in gratitude.

  — When have you seen someone—or when have you yourself been—trapped by the myth of "positive self-esteem"? In your example(s), which of the three problems with self-esteem listed above was the greatest threat?

  — Explain in your own words why seeing ourselves as *loved* is better than seeing ourselves as *good*.

- We are not advocating a return to "worm theology." Seeing ourselves as only dirty rotten sinners is just as unhelpful as seeing ourselves as faultless saints. We are both bearers of God's image and sinners. We are beautiful at times and not so pretty at other times. The real question is where the safety comes from that allows us to be all that we are. And the Bible's answer to that is love (1 John 4:18).

  — In what ways has God's love for you meant safety to be both sinner and saint? In what ways is God's love moving you from sinner to saint?

— What, if anything, are you doing now to teach your teenager about God's transforming love? What would you like to be doing?

• In speaking against "positive self-esteem," we're not saying that kids should not be praised for doing well. Children were created with a need for parental approval, so praise them for a job well done. Validating your teenagers' ability to do something consolidates a feeling of competency in them and helps them internalize that feeling.

— When has justifiable praise motivated you? If you can, think of an example from your teenage years.

 — What chance to validate your teenagers' ability to do something can you expect to have this week? When that opportunity comes, praise them for a job well done.

Do not buy into the philosophy that building positive self-esteem is the answer to all of a teenager's problems. Your teens need, most of all, to feel loved as they are and then to be encouraged to learn how to do things well. The issue of "Am I good enough?" will become a non-issue. A "loved self" is much more secure than a "good self" any day.

The Cure: Safe Enough to Be Real (page 118)

Making teenagers feel bad does not motivate them to do better. Nor does making them feel good guard them from all of life's pitfalls. The answer to the self-esteem problem is this: Give them a combination of grace and truth, and they will feel safe enough to be real.

• What aspect of yourself, if any, did you feel you had to hide when you were growing up? What made you feel that way? What can parents do to keep their teenagers from feeling they need to hide a part of themselves? Specifically, what are you doing in this regard?

- Kids of all ages need to learn what (hopefully) their parents have already learned: they need to know that it is okay to fail, to hurt, or to be less than perfect. They need to feel secure in bringing their bad parts to relationship.

— What are you doing to teach your teenagers that it is okay to fail and to be less than perfect? Think about the behaviors they see in you as well as the words they hear from you.

— What are you doing to teach your teens that it is okay to hurt? What do they see about how you deal with hurt? What do they receive and hear from you when they are hurt?

There is no problem that the grace and guidance of loving parents cannot get teenagers through. But if teenagers do not feel they can be who they really are, then their problems never get solved. They just get hidden away to grow into bigger cancers.

The Process of Embracing Reality (page 119)

How do you teach your teenagers to live in an imperfect world? You start by forcing them to face reality and giving them enough grace to embrace reality and to move on. Let's take a closer look at this process.

• ***Protest:*** The first thing a teenager (or an adult!) will do is protest the painful reality. Give an example of a time when reality hit your teens. In what ways did they (quite naturally) protest that reality, be it the pain of separation (breaking up with a boyfriend or girlfriend), discipline (having to stay home Saturday night after breaking curfew Friday night), or something else?

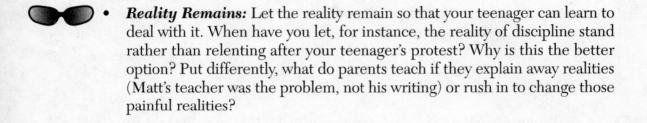 • ***Reality Remains:*** Let the reality remain so that your teenager can learn to deal with it. When have you let, for instance, the reality of discipline stand rather than relenting after your teenager's protest? Why is this the better option? Put differently, what do parents teach if they explain away realities (Matt's teacher was the problem, not his writing) or rush in to change those painful realities?

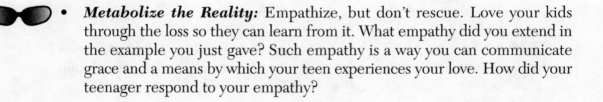 • ***Metabolize the Reality:*** Empathize, but don't rescue. Love your kids through the loss so they can learn from it. What empathy did you extend in the example you just gave? Such empathy is a way you can communicate grace and a means by which your teen experiences your love. How did your teenager respond to your empathy?

• ***Grief:*** Whatever the hurt, with enough reality and empathy, adolescents will mourn and let it go. Consider again your teenager's response to the empathy you offered. What evidence of mourning and then of letting go did you see? Be specific.

- ***Problem Solving and Resolution:*** Resolution involves finding out what we did wrong, fixing it to the extent possible, and in any case, continuing on. So, still working with your example, what did you do to help your teenager learn why she failed and to encourage her to try again? If the example was in the area of performance, did your teen "get back on the horse and try again"? If the example was in the area of relationship, did your teenager "confront, repent, forgive, and reconcile"?

Not pain, sin, failure, or anything else can stop us if we have reality, comfort, the ability to grieve, and the courage to go on. Our God is one who brings forth victory from any defeat. And if we lose well, we can be victorious, too. This is one of the best lessons your teenager can ever learn: There is no loss in life great enough that facing the truth with grace and having the courage to go forward cannot cure.

Some Examples (page 123)

In the various stages of childhood (infancy, toddlerhood, early childhood, adolescence), the formula of facing the truth with grace and having the courage to go forward is the same, but the content changes. Let's consider adolescence.

- In adolescence, the good-bad split gets reawakened. Adolescents test out new aspects of themselves. Dating is a whole new world that will bring the roller-coaster ride of "Am I good enough?" Don't be surprised at the up-and-down nature of these years.

  — What can you do to be there for your teenagers as they process the pain and the victories of these volatile years? Be specific.

- Youth pastors, coaches, teachers, and other trusted adults can offer teenagers safety. What safe places do your teens have to process their feelings?

- Limits help with integration—if you hold to them.

— When have you felt your teenagers' hatred because, as you've held to appropriate rules and limits, you've thwarted their desires? And when have you sensed your teenagers' love for the safety you provide?

- Why is it important to not get controlling or aggressive about the limits you set? What can you do to keep from getting caught up in power struggles with your teens as they try to integrate all that they feel about those limits?

— What truths help you stand strong when your teenager rages and protests against you and the limits you hold to?

Inasmuch as possible, make it safe for your teenagers to talk to you. But give them other places to integrate as well. And remember that if you do not get controlling or aggressive, they will be able to internalize your limits.

Being Hated (page 126)

One of the most important qualities for a parent to possess is the ability to be hated. Your kids will never integrate their good and bad feelings if you are uncomfortable with their anger toward you.

- What did you do with feelings of hatred for your parents? If you shared them, how did they respond? Was their response helpful or not? Explain.

- How do you want to respond to your teenagers' feelings of hatred toward you when you set a limit they don't like? Remember the importance of holding firm and offering grace.

The Result (page 127)

If all goes well with this process of embracing reality (protest, reality re-mains, accept reality, grief, resolution), you will build several things into your teenagers' character that will last them a lifetime.

• Review the list of character traits on page 127 of the text.

— Which traits might you need to work on so that you can be sure you are passing them on to your teenagers?

— What traits do you see hints of or perhaps even strongholds of in your teenager?

The character traits you just reviewed will enable your teenagers to live a good life—not a perfect life, but a good and satisfying life. Every day, inching toward perfection and never getting there, they will enjoy the process. If that happens, you will have done a very good job of helping them live in reality.

In the next chapter we will look at some of those realities.

Hands-on Exercise

If You Do One Thing Besides Pray . . .

Key to countering the popular cultural myth of "positive self-esteem" is teaching kids about God's love—and remembering that you are modeling it in all your interactions with them. Earlier you were asked, "What are you doing to continue to teach your teenager about God's love? What would you like to be doing?" This week act on one of your ideas.

Also look for an opportunity to praise your teen for a job well done (such as keeping curfew, balancing studies and extracurricular activities, getting chores done without a lot of reminders, being respectful to parents and siblings). Remember that kids need their parents' approval, so when they do a job well, let them know of your approval. Validating their ability to do something consolidates a sense of competency in teenagers and helps them internalize that sense. At the same time, remember to validate what is done with excellence or great effort, rather than praising your teens when they do what is required and no more. Don't set your teens up to expect their future boss to throw a party when they show up to work on time.

Folded-Hands Exercise

"My help comes from the LORD . . ."

—PSALM 121:2

Almighty God, your Son was very direct: "In the world you have tribulation." Yet still the hard stuff can surprise us, and we can struggle to accept reality—the reality about ourselves, about others, and about the world around us. I think of the loss I've experienced, and I don't look forward to the losses that my kids will know in their lives. But I realize that being able to face reality—to acknowledge and address our imperfections, our failures, our losses—is key to growth and the development of strong character.

As I continue to help my teenagers learn and accept that they are not perfect, may I use those opportunities to also teach them about your love. Use me, Lord God, so that the issue of "Am I good enough?" will become a non-issue for my kids. May they know that they are loved—and may I see in their lives that a "loved self" is much more secure than a "good self" any day.

Thank you that my teenager and I can both rest in your love that accepts us now even as your Spirit works in us to transform us and make us more like Christ—in whose name we pray. Amen.

Seven

Developing Gifts and Talents
Competence

Parenting Principles

- Developing competence and skill in certain areas helps kids take their place in, and contribute to, the adult world.
- Parents need to show their kids that work is good, important, and expected.
- Parents need to help kids develop competency areas as well as learn the disciplines of work.

Remember how Ryan quietly explained body design, sanding, wheel polishing, and axle positioning to several Pinewood Derby competitors, fathers as well as sons? Showing a great command of his subject, he gave examples and showed alternatives, and those who learned from him had faster cars than previous years. Now, Ryan will probably not race derby cars full-time when he grows up—but he is well on his way to taking his place in the workforce, equipped to excel.

Your Child Is a Working Child (page 129)

Work is a central aspect of our existence. God designed us not only to be in relationship and to connect, but to be productive in the world, to contribute meaningfully to others in a significant way.

- Much of the time and energy invested in living involves some work. In which of the following areas is your teenager working? Give a few specific examples.

  — Life skills (hygiene, clothing, finances, time management, home maintenance)

— School (junior high or high school, Sunday school or youth group)

— Sports

— Technical hobbies

— Extracurricular activities (Scouts, music, dance, etc.)

- Kids who grow up competent in something are better able to function in the adult world, where expertise is a large part of life. They will have more to offer, and they will gain more satisfaction from executing their craft well.

  — As a child, what kind of encouragement toward competence did you receive—or how were you discouraged or held back?

  — What, if anything, did you become competent in—or begin to become competent in—as a child or teenager? How has that experience served you well—or how has its absence been something of a handicap?

Competence is the area of character growth we will be discussing in this chapter. We will tell you how you can help your teenagers continue to develop the capacity to be experts in some area, to perform well as craftspeople, and to contribute meaningfully through their gifts and abilities.

Competence: Entrance into the "Adult Club" (page 130)

Teaching teenagers competence helps them move toward adulthood. In a way, adults form an exclusive club—it's not open to all who want to join. The club has requirements for membership. To meet those requirements, teens should now be well on the way toward establishing both good work habits and core competency areas, that is, areas of skill in which they are developing expertise. After all, they will soon be required to be good workers either in college or the job world.

- The first requirement is to be competent in some area. Teenagers need to have a function or service to offer to the adult club (Proverbs 22:29).

    — Learning to master some ability is part of the process of bringing teenagers into the adult world. When did you find that your competence in some area meant entrance into the adult club? Be specific.

    — Teens know that doing things well is something that brings them praise and good things (such as friends with common interests or greater opportunities). Think of some ways you can help your teenager see that competence in computers, science, art, literature, or the like is a good thing.

- The second requirement for entrance into the adult world is to become equal and mutual with adults. Kids have moms and dads as a safety net when they fail. Grown-ups must do things for themselves without a safety net.

    — In what ways are you a safety net for your teenager? Be specific.

    — Teenagers' need for their parents shifts from their human parents to God himself, who wants to be their only parent (Matthew 23:9). What did your parents do, if anything, to facilitate this transition in your life?

— What would you like to do to help your teens continue shifting their dependence from you to God their heavenly Father?

• The third requirement for adulthood is relational. Adults connect on both a bonding and a task level. Developing some skill or expertise helps your teenager relate in both ways to other adults.

— When has some skill or expertise helped you connect to another adult?

— When has your teenager connected with a peer on the basis of a shared interest? What indication of increased confidence or enjoyment, if any, did you see in your child during that interaction?

The ability of teenagers to master some gift or talent is an important source of a realistic self-image and confidence. As they "own" some interest and grow in it, they are able to experience life less as helpless, dependent infants and more as grown-ups (Proverbs 13:19 KJV).

Love and Approval Are Different (page 131)

Kids of any age should not have their love needs tied to their performance. Your kids should be secure in their relationship with you—no strings attached. This is the essence of grace: love that one doesn't deserve.

• Depending on how your parents separated (or didn't separate) love and approval, what did you learn about hard work and love when you were growing up?

• What are you doing—or could you be doing—to keep love and approval separate for your teenager? In what ways are you saying, "I love you with no strings attached. However, I don't approve of how you are handling the jobs we are giving you"?

Remember, keep love and approval separate. As a parent, you need to be "for" your teenagers no matter how good, bad, industrious, or lazy they are.

Work Is Good, Important, and Expected (page 132)

Helping kids develop competency first involves helping them create a "pro-work" attitude. You need to provide an environment in which they can internalize the reality that work—both inside and outside the home—is good, important, and expected.

• What are you and your spouse modeling for your teens about attitude, responsibility, energy, and enthusiasm as one or both of you head off to work?

• What are you and your spouse modeling for your teenagers about attitude, responsibility, energy, and enthusiasm as you tackle the tasks of keeping a home running (such as gardening, cooking, cleaning, laundry, washing cars)?

If they haven't already, teenagers need to make friends with work and to understand that it is just as much a part of life as attachment, friends, and fun. Your job is to help structure, focus, and deepen their involvement in their work.

Work and Skill Are Part of Life (page 133)

Your teenagers need to see you involved in your work and bringing the interesting part of it to the family conversation. They need to internalize an emotional picture of someone who is mastering some niche in life. So model interest in, involvement in, even frustration with your work both inside and outside the home.

- **Values:** Your work is, at some level, tied into your values. Talk to your teenagers about why you do what you do and why you think it's important.

  — What kind of tasks within the home do you do, and why do you think they are important?

  — What kind of work outside the home, if any, do you do, and why do you think it is important?

   — What do you think your teenager understands about why you do what you do and why you think it's important?

- **Habits:** Model your work ethics and habits. Provide a picture of an industrious person who plays well, relates well, and works well. Expect the same from your teenager.

  — What are you teaching-by-doing about being on time, finishing tasks, and following instructions?

   — What household tasks are your teenagers responsible for? What consequences are appropriate for work not completed without supervision?

- **Attitudes:** Grumbling has been a part of work life ever since the Fall. So you can't ask teenagers to whistle while they work, but you can require them to keep their protests respectful. Teens also need to appreciate the value of what they're doing. The goal is to have kids move from being dependent on praise to knowing the inner satisfaction that comes with a job well done.

— Consider the grumbling you do (if any). What attitude toward work are you modeling?

— What are you doing to show your teenagers that you appreciate their efforts to work around the house (helping in the kitchen, washing the cars, working in the yard, keeping their rooms picked up, caring for younger siblings, and the like)?

• **Normalization:** Normalize work both inside and outside the home for your teenagers. Let them know that you expect them to work most of their lives.

— In which of your words and behaviors, if any, does your teenager see you living for weekends and vacation? Why is that a bad model?

— What work around the house reminds your teenager that work is a normal and ongoing aspect of life? Be specific.

• **Delegation:** Teenagers should be shouldering appropriately complex and difficult tasks.

— What tasks are appropriate for your teenager?

— What kind of commentary about those tasks will remind your teenager that the family is a team and the team works together?

• **Work and Money:** We don't believe in paying a child for chores. We suggest instead that, on a regular basis, you give your teenagers some money not tied to chores.

— What are the benefits (long- and short-term) of this approach to work and money?

— What kind of program for tithing, saving, and spending have you implemented—or would you like to implement—with your teens? Take a few minutes either to evaluate the current program or to develop a program and then plan how to implement it.

• **Skill:** In work, it's not enough to show up and participate. Results do matter. Help your teenager value skill and achievement.

— What problems can result from parents demanding too much? from parents being afraid to challenge their child? Which extreme (if either) did you grow up with, and what were the effects?

— What can you do to be sure you're not asking either too little or too much of your teenager? What resources and reality checks can you consult?

- ***Creativity and Problem Solving:*** The heart of work is creating good things and solving problems. Getting teenagers involved in tasks is inviting them to these fundamental aspects of work.

 — In what aspects of their homework, chores, and outside jobs (we support outside jobs in the teen years) can you encourage your teenager to be creative?

 — What can you do (or not do!) so that your teenager finds himself in the role of problem solver as he, for instance, tackles a challenging homework assignment or faces a scheduling dilemma? In what ways, for instance, can you empathize with the difficulty of the problem but not rescue him and keep him from learning by doing the task at hand? What benefit comes to your teenager when you empathize rather than do the task for him?

- ***Evaluation:*** It helps kids to be graded on their performance. They need to experience success and failure. Being graded helps them monitor their ways and make necessary corrections. It reinforces responsibility and punishes slothfulness.

— Why isn't it helpful to eliminate failure from a teenager's experience?

 — What does it mean to you to "fail well"—and what will you do to continue to help your teen fail well?

- **Competition:** Mastering tasks often involves some conflict with and comparison to other children. Help your teenager know how to compete well.

    — What does "competing well" mean to you? What have you taught—or would you like to teach—your teenagers about how to compete well and how to accept loss?

    — What are you modeling about competition? about how to compete? and about how to accept loss? In what scenes from your life can your teenager see you valuing relationship above competition?

    — In what areas of life is your teenager competing? What good things are coming from that competition?

- **Fears of Success and Failure:** Kids of all ages will most likely struggle with fears of both doing well and of failing in life. These two different struggles have much to do with their relationship with you as the parent.

    — As a child, did you fear success? Did you fear failure? If you answered yes to either question, how has that fear affected your life (and maybe still affects it)?

    — How can the unconditional love of their parents help keep these fears from taking root and later even incapacitating teens?

— What evidence of failure anxiety, if any, have you noticed in your teenager? What steps will you take to repair this fear? In what setting would she be most likely to talk with you about what she is scared of? How will you reassure her of your unconditional love, or that you won't become angry, or that you also make mistakes? What opportunities to grow in this area can you give your teenager?

Work and skill are part of life, and you can do much to continue to help your teenager embrace work and succeed.

Developing Talents and Gifts (page 139)

Not only do you want to help your teenagers learn how to integrate work into their lives, but you also want to help them with the specific interests, talents, gifts, and aptitudes God put into them in potential form. Parenting involves helping your teens explore, discover, and develop those capacities that they will later enjoy and excel in.

- ***Discovering Talents:*** Within the soul of every kid are certain aptitudes waiting to emerge and bloom into talents and gifts. God has done his job, and your job is to invite your teenagers to engage in various experiences so that you and they can figure out what they value, excel in, and love doing.

  — Through the years, what have you seen your teenager love and excel in? What have you done and perhaps are even doing now to encourage those talents and gifts?

  — What are you doing to continue to give your teenager opportunities to find new loves and to discover hidden talents in such areas as sports, the arts, the sciences, church involvement, and helping others?

- **Development:** Invite your teens to continue to discover their interests. And when they latch onto some interest and have invested time and energy in it, challenge them to develop their talent. Help them to deepen their involvement and mastery.

    — What lessons on encouraging your kids to discover and pursue their interests does your own experience offer? Jot down some ideas of things you want to do and maybe even don't want to do to help your teenagers move from interest to competency.

    — What challenges do you expect to face as you continue to encourage your teens to master a particular skill? What, for instance, will you say when she wants to quit music lessons? What will you do if he is kicked off a team for being disruptive?

- **The Basics:** All the while that you are guiding your teens toward mastery in specialty areas, they should also be gaining competency in the universal areas of life that all adults need—areas such as academics, problem solving, social skills, language, hygiene and health, and home maintenance.

    — Why might it be easy for parents of a teenager gifted in some area to neglect these basic life skills? Why is that unwise and detrimental to the teen?

    — What are you doing—and what could you be doing—to help your teenager gain greater competence in the following areas? Be specific.

    Academics

Problem solving

Social skills

Language

Hygiene and health

Home maintenance

- ***The Parent as Background:*** Understand your parental role in helping kids develop mastery. You are in the background, providing a structure for them to experience growth. Don't get caught feeling that your success is measured by your kids' success.

   — Review the four words of caution listed on page 142 of the text. Which of the errors pointed out here have you seen or experienced? What resulted in the life of the teenager who suffered under these parental mistakes?

   — To which of these four dangers might you be most vulnerable as you parent your teenager? Think now about how to prevent this behavior.

*It is a great calling to help your kids find and grow competent in both spe-
cial areas and life's tasks. Keep picturing them as adults in whom you are investing time to help them prepare for entering the adult world.*

Ages and Stages (page 142)

*Kids are always working on something. They have God-given blueprints
geared toward mastering life. Review the table on page 143 of the text, paying
particular attention to the Adolescence and College sections.*

- What evidence do you see that your teenager is indeed working on these
  age-appropriate tasks?

- What items listed suggest that you could be helping your teen master some
  of these basic tasks? What specific steps will you take?

*As you watch your teenagers master these age-appropriate tasks and en-
courage and assist along the way, you are preparing them to enter the adult
world as competent and confident adults.*

Creating a Workaholic? (page 144)

*Some parents fear that modeling, inviting, and challenging adolescents to
work will result in adults who are addicted to their jobs and have no other life.
However, a healthy, involved parent doesn't cause workaholism. If attachment,
responsibility, and reality are all in their proper perspective in the child's character development, work capacities find their own place inside the child.*

- Workaholics often find in their work respite from their fears of closeness,
  their inability to make attachments, their problems in setting limits with
  others, and their anxieties about failure. How can healthily involved parenting help a teenager avoid these fears?

- Parents can't give what they don't have. How healthy is your approach to work? How balanced is your life? Does work help meet any unresolved needs or offer relief from the kinds of fears listed above? In essence, what are you modeling for your teen?

Mastery of work is one of the most rewarding aspects of parenting because it provides you with an opportunity to see measurable growth. But a working child isn't necessarily a moral child. In the next chapter we will take a look at the important character task of conscience development.

Hands-on Exercise

If You Do One Thing Besides Pray . . .

Even if your teenagers' junior high or high school doesn't offer a career planning course or job-shadowing experience, you can provide the same benefits by partnering with them for success in high school and beyond. What skills and abilities have your teens demonstrated? What interests do they have? What career paths do these things point to? Help your teenagers first identify possible career options (high school counselors may have tools available) and then arrange interviews with people working in areas of interest. Take your teens to work with you. Set up a community service project that offers some experience in a field of interest. And make sure that your teens are on the academic path that prepares them for the career they're seeking or at least keeps options open for them.

Folded-Hands Exercise

"My help comes from the LORD . . ."

—PSALM 121:2

Almighty God, the truth that love and approval are different things is a powerful one, and it's one that your love helps me understand. You love me even when I sin, when I do and say things that you in your holiness don't approve of. I ask you to teach me to love my kids with that kind of unconditional love. May I point them to your standards and mine for them, but may they always rest in our love.

I also ask you to give me wisdom and insight regarding my kids' unique personalities and interests, talents and skills. Guide me as I guide my teens toward mastery and competence, toward classes they need to take and career possibilities to which you may be calling them. Most of all, work in them the desire to do what you would have them do with the skills, the abilities, and the years you have given them. I pray in Jesus' name. Amen.

Eight

Making a Conscience
Morality

┌─ **Parenting Principles** ─────────────────────────┐

- A sense of moral awareness arises from several elements, which together form a mature conscience.
- The purpose of the conscience is both to protect love and to align itself with God's reality.
- Kids develop conscience through identification, imitation, modeling, and experience.

└──┘

How is a teen's conscience developed to maturity? Can it be injured? Can it be healed? Are there better ways to develop a conscience than others? What should you focus on as you think about moral development in your teenagers? What morals are important? We will look at these issues in this chapter on conscience and morals.

What Is a Conscience? (page 146)

Defining conscience is complicated for biblical theologians as well as psychologists. A sense of moral awareness includes:

An understanding of right and wrong
The morals that will guide your child
An internal ability to weigh moral decisions
An ability to self-correct
A proper internal response to violating a standard
A desire to do right

- Where does the sense of right or wrong in someone's conscience come from? What are you to feel when your standard is violated? Is your standard automatically right? Can you have a "wrong standard" in your conscience? Why are these questions important for you as a parent to consider?

If your teenager enters adulthood with the above list, you will have done well. Let's look at how parents can develop their child's moral awareness, what gets in the way, and what will help.

Three Big Things Worth Worrying About (page 147)

Parents worry. And the problem is not that parents worry; it's what parents worry about. Three things worth worrying about are that your kids develop a conscience, the tone of the conscience, and the content and quality of the conscience.

IS IT TOO LATE?

Every teenager has a conscience, but the stage of development among teens can vary widely. If your teens have few moral standards, don't pay attention to moral rules, or behave in other ways that suggest an underdeveloped conscience, you can still do much to help that conscience grow.

- With empathy for your teenagers, define moral parameters for their behavior and provide clear consequences for violating those parameters. Doing so will enable your teens to experience that there is a law of reality external to them and to learn that, if they ignore that law of reality, they will experience great pain.

- Giving your teens this context will enable them to internalize the law of reality and make it part of their system of morals, replacing their "law of the jungle"/"me first" stance.

- Move your teenagers from this moral stance of simply doing the right thing to the higher ground of acting according to the law of love and empathy for others. Challenge their thinking with "You're treating others this way. This behavior hurts them, and you would be hurt if they behaved like that toward you. You will have certain consequences so that you can learn to see your hurtful influence on others and to act kindly because you care about people."

- **That They Develop a Conscience:** "Moral development" refers to kids developing both a moral awareness of right and wrong and the inclination to follow in the right direction and enforce internal consequences if they do wrong.

  — The parents' first task is to let their kids know right from wrong. Setting limits for their kids—things that parents will allow and things they don't—can start sometime around the end of the child's first year, and parents continue to set limits as their child grows. What limits have you set for your teenager?

  — Explain in your own words why your no is a good thing.

  — Are you at risk of setting too many rules? How can you consolidate or simplify the rules? Are you being too rigid to avoid being too lax? What might be a happy medium?

  — A rule without enforcement teaches teenagers that they are above the law and that morals are just suggestions. Are you consistent in your enforcement of the rules? What keeps you from being as consistent as you like? What help can you get if you'd like to be more able to discipline and follow through on consequences?

- **The Tone of the Conscience:** The tone of a teenager's conscience will determine, to some degree, whether that teenager will follow it. Parents can build morals within their teens, but if the tone of the teen's conscience is angry, guilt-producing, and condemning, that conscience becomes the adversary.

  — The Bible teaches that we can live under the law (obey—or incur wrath, condemnation, and loss of love) or under grace (know love, forgiveness, and nurturing). What emotional tone are you offering your teenagers when you discipline them? Review the descriptions of the tone of the law and the tone of grace (pages 149–50 in the text) before you answer this question.

  — Does your teenager's conscience seem more friend or enemy? Give specific evidence to support your answer. If you're not sure, is that a problem or not? Explain.

- **The Content and Quality of the Conscience:** A teenager's moral awareness should be a gracious and loving enforcer, but what are the laws of the land? On what are you going to focus? What kind of content is going to be written on your teen's heart? The content changes as kids grow up, but here are a few key principles for any age.

  — The Bible always teaches morality in the bigger context of rejecting God, hurting oneself, and hurting others. So *focus on the "whys" behind the rules; teach teens that their behavior affects others*. To a teenager late for dinner, say, "Out of respect for the other members of the family, we will go ahead and eat without you so your tardiness affects only you and not other people." A teenage boy should hear that it grieves God for him to have premarital sex, to have him love his own impulses more than God. Also, is he considering what he is doing to the young woman? to her future husband? And does he realize that he is hurting himself?

In what situations with your teenager can you focus on the "why" behind the rule? Be specific.

 — Morals are not killjoys. *Morals are to protect our lives and to ensure a good life.* They are the principles that undergird success in life, and reality teaches that truth. Reality consequences, instead of anger, guilt, and alienation, teach kids that God's laws are there for a reason. *"If I do wrong, I suffer,"* a kid learns. What are some of the reality consequences you use—or could use—in disciplining your teenager?

— Parents need to teach the principle of wisdom. Wisdom teaches that there are positive and negative reasons for any moral law, that life works best when you live it as it was designed and doesn't work when you don't live it as it was designed. In what typical or frequent parenting situation can you be teaching wisdom? Be specific (e.g., diligence makes people successful; lying destroys relationships; drugs fry your brain and ruin your life; sleeping around can kill you; cheating lands you in jail)—and then teach it.

The content of the conscience has changed as your teenagers have grown up. Ideally, your teens are moving toward protecting relationships with God and others, as well as aligning themselves with the reality of God's created order. If you focus more on relationship, reality issues, and reality consequences than on petty rules, you will help your teenagers move toward a life of producing and protecting love as well as being able to function in reality.

The Process (page 154)

Moral functioning is developmental, just like God's revelation to humankind: God gave the law to the children of Israel, and then in Jesus he fulfilled it with the principle of love and internal motivation.

- Review the discussion of growth in morality and the four-step progression (page 155 of the text). Why are consequences important in the shaping of a conscience?

- What evidence do you see, if any, that your teenager is beginning to understand morality on a fundamental level?

Giving consequences forms a child's conscience and helps with some of the irrational thinking involved in the "bad happening = I'm bad" morality. Kids learn right from wrong based on what happens when they do a or b. The corresponding idea of when "Mom or Dad is pleased, or not" slowly translates into "My conscience is pleased, or not."

Your Own Ten Commandments (page 156)

Kids build values and morality in the context of relationship. Your laws, as you teach them and as you live them, are being written on their hearts. Through the years, these laws become part of their consciences through identification, imitation, modeling, and experience.

- ***Identification*** is the process by which kids take in their parents at a very unconscious level. They identify with their parents as moral agents. They feel your attitudes toward things, and those attitudes will likely become part of them. Which of your attitudes (both positive and negative) toward what things have you seen your teenager take in through the years?

- **Imitation** is more active: kids will imitate your behavior to learn how to behave. What ways of speaking, gesturing, and, especially at this age, dealing with situations (frustration, anger) has your teenager learned from you?

- **Modeling** is the taking on of roles and abilities, such as the role of being male or female and the ability to treat people nicely or poorly.

  — In what ways are you showing your teenager how to be a moral person? Be specific.

  — In what aspects of your life, if any, are you saying one thing but doing another?

- Kids will imitate you, and they will also **experience** you directly. Just as God gave his family (the children of Israel) a set of commandments to follow, parents give their family their own set. It is given not in stone, but with experience.

  — Remember the examples of relational theology some people learned growing up? (See page 157 of the text.) What would you add to the list? Which items, if any, are lessons you learned?

  — Now consider yourself as parent. What relational theology have you taught your teenager through the years?

— Two parents form a conscience. If both parents are not on the same page, a kid gets a "split conscience." How much in sync have you and your spouse been as you've served as the external conscience for your children? How much in sync are you during these teenage years? Where do you need to be more in line with one another—in tone? in content? in quality? What will you do to improve your alignment? Be specific.

Remember, no matter what you believe, how you relate to your kids is forming their conscience. Their brains are recording as rules your responses to them.

Some Good Values (page 159)

Review the list of good values to instill in your kids (page 159 in the text). The Bible teaches that these are the basic values that life in God is built upon. Consider each value listed.

- What are you teaching your teenagers about each value through your words—and what do you want to be teaching them? What will you do to teach those lessons?

- What are you teaching your teenagers about each of these values by your actions—and what do you want to be teaching them? What will you do to teach those lessons?

In the final analysis, conscience is an important aspect of parenting. But to just give a teenager rules falls short of a biblical view of conscience. Make sure that rules are focused on love, corrected by love, and built in the context of love. If they are, your teen will one day thank you for all the discipline along the way.

In the next chapter we will look at the deepest morality: a teenager's connection to God.

Hands-on Exercise

If You Do One Thing Besides Pray . . .

Make an appointment or grab a cup of coffee with a dad or mom farther down the parenting road whose teenagers or adult children are leading godly, moral lives. Get some tips from them. Learn from their mistakes. And ask any parenting questions you may have.

Folded-Hands Exercise

"My help comes from the LORD . . ."

—PSALM 121:2

Almighty God, you are clear in your Word that there are two ways of living—under the law or under grace. I ask you to help the tone in our home to be one of grace, and I acknowledge that I can't do that without your Spirit working in me. Be at work, I pray, transforming the angry, harsh, condemning, guilt-producing, and alienating words and ways I have and the danger of withholding love from my teenagers based on their performance. And, Father, replace those with manifestations of your grace—with an ability to be loving, nurturing, and forgiving, to offer an unconditional love that builds relationship and empowers my children. I need you and the wisdom you can provide me as I face the challenge of making a healthy and godly conscience in my almost-adult children. I pray in Jesus' name. Amen.

——— Nine ———

Connecting to God
Worship and Spiritual Life

┌ Parenting Principles ────────────

- A teenager's spiritual life needs to be centered around connecting to God as the Author of reality.
- Parents need to present to their teens spiritual life integrated with everyday life.
- Parents need to teach teenagers the spiritual disciplines and give them experiences to internalize them.

Concerned not only about the cultural and political shifts of the late sixties but the spiritual problems as well, my [John's] dad volunteered to teach Sunday school to the teens in our church. Like him, you may have a deep desire to encourage your teenagers in their spiritual life, but you wonder where to begin. This chapter resolves this tension by dealing with two aspects—being involved and having a structure under which to operate.

Character and Spirituality (page 162)

A child's spiritual life is a fundamental part of total character development. Remember that growing character will help your teenager function as an adult in the world.

- Adolescents demand that life adapt to them, while mature adults adapt themselves to the realities of life. So, to grow up, your teens need to order their lives around the Author of reality. God has designed your teenagers—and reality—to operate in certain ways within certain parameters. Finding and responding to God's statutes and ways becomes the key to growing up.

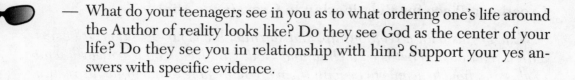

— What do your teenagers see in you as to what ordering one's life around the Author of reality looks like? Do they see God as the center of your life? Do they see you in relationship with him? Support your yes answers with specific evidence.

— As you were growing up, how did you learn God's statutes and ways—and how have you responded to them through the years?

• You may know loving, hardworking, and reality-based people who have no spiritual life or interests, who don't experience God as the source of life. You may also know highly religious folks who know the Bible well and use God talk, but their everyday lives don't reflect what they know. For them, the center of what makes them tick is not connected to the rest of "real" life.

— What might a parent do to contribute to each of these two possibilities?

— What might a parent do to prevent these two possibilities and raise a child who experiences God as the source of life, whose everyday life reflects a personal knowledge of Jesus?

Parents cannot separate their teenager's spiritual life from the rest of life. Our spiritual life is meant to be integrated into all the aspects of our relationships and tasks. Spiritual character growth therefore involves much more than religious training; it involves helping a teenager experience that the essence of existence is spiritual.

Creating a Place for Relationship to Grow (page 163)

Life begins with a relationship, and spiritual life is no exception. It begins with a relationship between a child and God. Children who learn early who God is and how he wants to be with them are more able to integrate his reality into the rest of their years. But it's never too late for a child to learn this truth.

- A relationship requires two willing parties. Parents can't force a teenager to develop a relationship with God. God invites but does not force himself on you or your teen (Revelation 3:20).

  — God has arranged things so that kids have a voice as to when they are ready to address him. Why is this both sobering and freeing?

  — The parents' task is to do background work for their child's encounter with God, to create a context that fosters connectedness to God. Before looking closely at some ways to do so, consider what you may be doing now to create optimal conditions for your teenager to meet and love— or to continue to love and serve—God (Hebrews 11:6). Give a few examples from your everyday life as a parent.

- ***Seeing the Eternal in the Everyday:*** Teenagers need to approach life as if it were eternal; this is fundamental in the quest for God.

  — What are you doing—or could you do to—help your teenagers see the eternal in the everyday parts of life? What about your day or their day can you point to? Where do you see the eternal in the everyday? Consider answers to prayers, evidence that God is helping them know and do the right thing, and times when a sermon exactly fits the circumstances in their life. Ask the Lord to give you as well as your teens eyes to see his active presence and involvement in daily life.

— Teenagers are able to understand that the rules in both the seen and the unseen worlds are similar, that principles such as love, faithfulness, honesty, and ownership work in both worlds. What current situation in your life gives you the opportunity to make this point? Also, spend some time asking the Lord to show you where you are not living in this world according to the rules of the unseen world, the rules and principles he established for both.

• ***Seeing God as the Source of All Good Things:*** Teens need to understand that while God wants them to follow his ways, he first wants to give them the good things they need.

— What opportunity might you have to reinforce for your teenager "that God is a better parent . . . than [you] are"? Why is that truth important?

— Teenagers benefit by seeing that you are a better parent by virtue of being connected to God. When has being in prayer, worship, or Bible study clearly given you what you need to better love and parent your teenagers? When, for instance, have you returned from church or prayer better able to listen, respond appropriately, or admit wrongdoing to them? Be specific about the time, and, in order to experience it regularly, note what helped make it especially significant for you and the Lord.

— What, if anything, has your teenager seen in you about how God gives good things (such as peace, hope, and strength) in the midst of hard times?

— In the last few weeks, when could your teenager have seen in your life that good things happen when people spend time with God, even though suffering happens, too?

- **Life Works Better Living It God's Way:** Teenagers need to experience God not only as Source, but also as King. God has structured reality according to certain truths, and he requires people to order their lives around his ways. The Bible contains those ways: truth exists in God's commands, laws, and principles for conducting our lives. Your teenagers need to understand and experience these truths (Psalm 1:2).

  — When have you experienced for yourself the truth that obedience to God's ways helps us, that spiritual growth and development both prosper and preserve life (Deuteronomy 6:24)? Be specific.

 — In what common situation in your teenagers' lives can you help them see that God's ways help us and that a life of obedience is a good thing? What will you do and say, for instance, the next time a drunk driving accident involving teenagers is in the paper or your teenager isn't honest about where she was spending her time? Also look for moments when you can talk about how God's "house rules" of love, fairness, faithfulness, and honesty make life work better in the same way that traffic lights and stop signs make the world safer and better.

— What are you doing regularly to get to know your Bible, Christian doctrine, and godly principles for living? What are you doing—or could you be doing—to encourage your teenager to know God's Word and his truth? What family worship or devotional time gives you the opportunity to read and discuss Bible passages? What age-appropriate Bible, devotional, and Bible studies have you found for your teen?

— Work on being able to verbalize to your teenager your beliefs and values. Why do you believe the Bible is true? Why does your family go to church? Why shouldn't people do drugs and have premarital sex? Go further than "Because God says so and he's the boss."

- ***The Spiritual Disciplines and Their Purpose:*** Parenting for spiritual growth involves more than teaching biblical truths and principles. It also involves helping teenagers internalize the disciplines of spiritual life. Spiritual disciplines, such as prayer, fellowship, and study, the memorization of and meditation on God's Word, are the traditional activities people of faith have entered into for many years as a way to connect with God.

    — What spiritual disciplines are a nurturing habit for you? Which ones do you need to better integrate in your life?

— What are you doing—and what else can you do—to practice the various spiritual disciplines with your teenagers? to encourage them to practice them on their own? What family mealtime rituals can you start? What special weekly time for family worship or devotionals have you or could you set into place? Most important, what are you doing to be sure to integrate the disciplines into daily life so that your kids understand why they're doing what they're doing?

— What are you doing to give your teenager the freedom he needs to work out his own relationship with God? Adolescents often need to find Christian churches and groups with which they can identify and that may not be the same as their parents. So help your teens get connected to a youth group and Sunday school that are biblically grounded but are more culturally similar to their style. Let your kids find their way to God in that context.

Your Faith Matters to Your Teen's Faith (page 169)

More than any other character capacity, spiritual development is caught more than taught. Children internalize more of what their parents are with God and with them than what their parents teach.

- What fellow believer can help you to see what kind of faith you model to people around you? Talk to that person about your strengths as well as your weaknesses and ask for prayer as you seek to lead a life of faith that you want your teenagers to desire and follow.

- If children have learned that Parents = God, they may leave God as they leave their parents. They may perceive God as someone from whom they must become independent in order to be a separate person. What can you do—or continue to do—to help keep your teenagers' experiences of you distinct from their experiences of God? You might want to talk to a parent whose kids are now godly adults.

- What stories of your own doubts, struggles with God, or failings to be the person you want to be have you shared—or could you share—with your teens? How do you let them see that a relationship with God, like a relationship with anyone, takes time, has conflict, and requires work?

Ask God to help your teenagers own their faith. That faith may be built on yours, but it was ultimately worked out by God and each of your teenagers.

The Image of God Issue (page 170)

Kids internalize experiences of their parents to form an image of God; however, other important factors (interpretation of life events, other realities, the ability to distinguish between human and divine, and change and growth) play a part in the development of a person's image of God.

- How did your impression of your parents form or impact your image of God for good and/or bad? What contributed to your growing beyond that image to a more mature and biblical understanding of God?

- People were created to seek and find God. What opportunities to draw close to God are you giving your teenager? What experiences (for example, driving them to youth group events) are you providing?

From Immature to Mature Dependency (page 171)

Your role of parent is temporary; God's is not. Your kids were designed to be God's kids forever (John 14:23). So you need to order your teens' earthly child-parent relationship differently than their heavenly one. While you are helping them to need you less, you are helping them need God more.

- What were some key events in your life that helped you transition from dependence on parents to dependence on the Lord? What lessons for parenting does your own experience provide you?

- The chart of age-appropriate capacities and spiritual needs (pages 172–74 of the text) shows what parents can do to help their kids shift from immature to mature dependency on God the Father. Look again at the Adolescence and College sections of the chart. Where, if at all, do you see your teenager in the description of an adolescent's faith? What do you learn about your role in the Parent's Tasks column? What encouragement do you find in the College section?

The Age of Faith? (page 174)

Parents struggle with the age-old question of when and how to help their child make a decision of faith. Only God knows a person's heart and readiness. As well, only he knows the hour and day that our lives will be required of us (Luke 12:20). And so parents need to rest in the reality of God's love, his deep and abiding love for their kids (2 Peter 3:9).

- What do you know about your teenager's faith? Has she accepted Jesus as her Lord and Savior? On what do you base your answer? If you're not sure if she has made an authentic commitment to Christ, what might you do to find out? If you're sure your teenager is not yet a believer, what might you do to encourage progress in that direction?

- If your teenager is rebelling against or questioning the Christian faith of his parents, what can you say if given the opportunity to address the following basic gospel truths? (Remember the guideline at this stage is "Teach less, dialogue more.")

   — The existence and love of God (as we've said, point out his involvement in your everyday life and comment on answered prayers).

   — The reality of our sinful state (adolescents know the struggle of wanting to do the right thing but being unable to do so).

   — The penalty of sin and God's provision through the death of Christ (death penalties in the news and Communion observances at church provide opportunities for dialogue).

   — The requirement of accepting Christ personally (talk about the difference between knowing *about* God and knowing God).

As you answer these questions, keep in mind the age-appropriate capacities and spiritual needs of your teenager (again see pages 172–74 in the text; also read the paragraph starting on the bottom of page 191 for more insight into teenagers and spirituality).

• A home where life in Christ is integrated with going to work, making dinner, taking out the trash, and interacting with family members is a good context for encouraging your children to commit themselves to Christ as their Savior and Lord. As we've touched on before, what evidence does your teenager see that your faith is integrated with your day-to-day life? Where does he see a disconnect?

• Be aware of your own emotional influence on your teenagers, especially in the arena of their freedom to choose. What are you doing to be sure that your teenagers know that their decision for or against Christ has nothing to do with your love and acceptance? If your teenagers are fighting to gain independence from you, how will that fact impact your role in their journey toward faith? What youth pastor or Christian peers can support your teenagers, wherever they are with the Lord?

• If your teenagers are not yet believers, pray for their salvation and ask God what your role might be in their spiritual growth at this point. Also spend some time thinking about how your teenagers are wired (for instance, is he private or outgoing? does she want to figure things out for herself or is she always teachable?) so that you will have a better idea of your role, even at this point in your teenagers' lives, in inviting them to name Jesus as Savior and Lord.

Your Father in heaven wants a relationship with your teenager. Ask him daily how you can help and when you need to get out of the way for this process to occur in his time.

Having considered the six character traits every child needs, we will now look at how parents are involved differently in different periods of their kids' lives. Part 3 focuses specifically on teenagers.

Hands-on Exercise

If You Do One Thing Besides Pray . . .

As we have stated, your faith matters to your child's faith. So work on strengthening your faith in the Lord so that you are walking your talk and modeling a vibrant faith in God that can be caught even as it is taught.

Where do you need to better walk your talk?

What regular Bible study/prayer group offers you support, accountability, and growth opportunities?

In what ways and at what times is worship a regular part of your life?

What regular prayer appointments with God do you keep?

In what ways are you serving the Lord and his people?

Who might serve as a spiritual mentor for you? Ideally that person is someone whose older children are walking with the Lord.

Ask the Lord to help you see the eternal in the everyday; to see him as the Source of all good things; and to live life his way.

Folded-Hands Exercise

"My help comes from the LORD . . ."

—PSALM 121:2

Almighty God, it's very sobering to realize that one's faith in you is more caught than taught. What have my teenagers seen in me and in my walk with you—and what are they seeing now? Teach me, I pray, to turn to you and depend on you in all areas of my life. Use the time I spend with you to make me a better parent. And help my relationship with you stay fresh, not become formal and stiff . . . my prayers real, not rote . . . and my Bible study a life-source, not a mere duty. Finally, Lord, I ask you to help my kids come to the point of owning their own faith—of coming to know you and love you and serve you—not merely piggybacking on my faith but coming to faith in Jesus because they have personally encountered you, wrestled with you, acknowledged their sin, and accepted your love. I pray in the name of Jesus, your ultimate gift of love to me and my children. Amen.

Part Three

Working Yourself Out of a Job

Preparing Them for Life on Their Own

Parenting Principles

- Adolescence is a reworking of past developmental issues in a new context.
- Parents need to set limits on how far a teen can go in working out these issues.
- The goal of adolescence is responsible independence, but parents need to be guiding the process.

My [Henry's] parents saw adolescence as a time-limited opportunity to prepare me to be on my own, and I'm grateful for what they did. Other parents, by their actions, say, "You are not on your own, so this is what you will do." And still others never offer any kind of parental limit.

- Consider where you fall along this spectrum of approaches to adolescence.

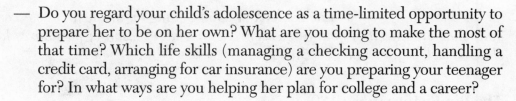

— Do you regard your child's adolescence as a time-limited opportunity to prepare her to be on her own? What are you doing to make the most of that time? Which life skills (managing a checking account, handling a credit card, arranging for car insurance) are you preparing your teenager for? In what ways are you helping her plan for college and a career?

— For whatever reasons, is your teen experiencing less freedom in adolescence than earlier in life? If so, what may be behind your becoming more of a police officer? What dangers are inherent in this approach?

 — Or, for whatever reasons, are you choosing to offer no limits at all during adolescence? Why is this perhaps easier alternative in the present a dangerous and unhealthy approach to parenting?

 — If, after considering the parenting path you're on, you've decided you'd like to change courses, what kind of resources and support can you turn to? (This workbook counts!)

 • More than anything else, parenting a teenager requires balance from Mom and Dad. Consider the balancing act reflected in the list on page 180 of the text. Which of these paradoxes have you encountered?

In this chapter we will take a look at what's going on inside an adolescent and what's required of you. Adolescence is indeed a season of paradoxes for child as well as for Mom and Dad.

The Big Picture (page 180)

To really understand adolescence, you need to stand back and understand first the big picture of how a child develops into an adult. Then you will understand adolescence as something both essential and important.

• Review "The Big Picture" overview of child development (pages 180–83).

— What reality check, if not hope or encouragement, did you find in this section?

— Adolescence is a second chance to fix things that need fixing. In light of that statement, what aspects of character in your teenager do you want to be sure to address?

Adolescence is a time when all of the past developmental issues (listed on page 182 of the text) are reworked in a different context. Your teenager will now work out those issues more independently in preparation for adulthood. Let's look at each of these six developmental functions in the adolescent years.

Trust and Dependency (page 183)

In teenagers, learning trust and dependency is more complicated than it is for an infant. Teenagers have to learn to depend and trust all over again in some major ways.

- First is the issue of trusting Mom and Dad. Adolescents feel connected when they feel understood. Validation of their experience is very important, and such affirmation comes less from lectures than from empathy. What words of empathy can you have ready for the next crisis in your teen's life?

- Teenagers also ask, "Can I lean on you without you robbing me of my independence?" If they are not able to go to you for guidance without being controlled, they will look for someone else to trust. Remember Shelly and her mom (pages 184–85)? What will you do to resist the impulse to try to control your teen's life?

- Trust for teens is also built through a parent's genuineness and congruence. Teenagers will see when you're not being real, not having integrity with your own agenda and feelings, or not being honest, and they won't trust you. Also, to put forth God as a way of controlling teens for a parent's own agenda is spiritual abuse. What changes in your behavior, if any, do these statements require?

- Don't be dismayed by your teenager's emerging tendency to put more trust in others than in you. Teens are also learning to trust in the romantic realm. Watch and observe. See if they are making good choices. Help them examine their relationships by asking questions (some are listed on page 186). Save your editorials for significant issues. You need to set boundaries on how much you will let your teenagers learn on their own. But as much as possible, stay away from control issues. If you have to go there, make sure that you give the reality reasons. What warnings in this perspective on adolescence do you appreciate? Which do you need to start acting on, and what steps will you take?

Independence and Autonomy (page 187)

One parent described adolescence as the terrible twos all over again, but this time in a bigger body. We personally don't see either time period as "terrible," but each one can be full of difficulty if you don't recognize the important stage of independence, separateness, and autonomy that a child is going through.

- Teenagers are moving away from their lifelong dependency on their parents. You can participate in your adolescent's emerging autonomy by being proactive. What can you do to give your teenager more autonomy in each of the following areas?

— Thinking for themselves and having their own opinions

— Questioning, evaluating, and choosing values

— Following their own desires and goals

— Building skills and abilities

— Looking ahead

— Developing their own spirituality

— Finding their own ways of making money

— Having parents available to them while they are working all of this out

• Review the conversation thirteen-year-old Sarah and her parents had as she entered the tumultuous teenage years (pages 188–89). Since then, Sarah's parents have partnered in her independence. What do you like about their approach? What elements can you adapt? What guidance do you find in the distinction between being a partner or an adversary in your teenager's inevitable independence?

- Partnering in independence and autonomy means to think always about your teenagers guarding and managing themselves at the appropriate level. Give them enough space to fail and then manage the failure with nurture, empowerment, support, discipline, and correction. Or, when they succeed, give them more freedom. Show them that responsible use of freedom leads to more freedom.

  — Your goal is to manage the process of independence in a way that leads to teenagers being able to manage themselves. Give them freedom within limits and require them to use it responsibly. In each of the following areas, what limits and requirements for responsibility are reasonable at this point in your teen's life?

    More freedom to go places and stay out later

    More freedom to do what they please without your being there all the time

    More freedom in choosing things they like instead of what you like

    Freedom to question things you have taught them and make up their own minds

    Freedom to pursue their own interests

Control over their likes and dislikes

More control over their spiritual life

- Expect your teenager to do some things that you don't like and that don't make sense just to express their independence from you. How do you want to respond when that happens—or happens again?

- It's a natural drive to say, "I know you don't like it, but I do." In light of that fact, what limits should you set on clothing? choice of friends? spiritual walk? Some ideas are given on pages 191–92.

  — In the spiritual realm, your teenagers might try to show independence as well. When have you seen parents and kids get into a power struggle over God? What can you do to avoid such a conflict? And what are you doing to expose your teens to good activities and good teaching in a good youth group with good youth leaders?

In short, you want your adolescents to develop independence. So give them areas in which they can be different from you that do not involve values. If you allow them to do this, they won't have to sacrifice more important areas of life to show you that they are their own person.

Limits and Authority (page 192)

It is important to let teenagers gradually become independent and more autonomous. But remember, they are not there yet! You are still around to protect them and manage them until they are ready. The problem is that they think they are ready now!

- As a parent of adolescents, you *must* be giving them more freedom. But freedom only has meaning within certain boundaries. Review the discussion of limits on pages 193–94 in the text. Which examples in each category are relevant to current parenting challenges? What boundaries does this discussion compel you to establish or continue to maintain? Be specific.

  — Reality limits

  — "Past-their-ability" limits

  — Moral, spiritual, and interpersonal limits

- Why is "freedom within limits" a good rule of thumb?

Just because teenagers don't like their parents' management doesn't make it unnecessary. You still have to give them limits and enforce the limits even as they want more and more freedom. When you consider imposing limits, ask yourself, "What is the danger here?" If the areas of reality danger, responsibility and faithfulness, or interpersonal relationships are violated, set limits and discipline.

In the next chapter, we will discuss specific things that many parents of teenagers ask about.

Hands-on Exercise

If You Do One Thing Besides Pray . . .

Trust and dependency, independence and autonomy, limits and authority—these are some of the developmental functions your teenager is addressing. Read about them again (starting on page 183 of the text). Note warnings about situations that you have not yet encountered as well as the steps you want to take and the words you want to remember to say when you do.

Also, it may be easier to talk to a teenager you're not related to! So hang out with a teen or college student, one who has his head on straight and his life headed in a healthy direction. Listen to what he says about what he wants—and doesn't want—from a parent at this stage of his life. Let him also give you a glimpse into his world—school, friendships, dating relationships, pressures, and his walk with the Lord. It could be an enlightening and helpful conversation.

Folded-Hands Exercise

"My help comes from the LORD . . ."

—PSALM 121:2

Lord, I find real comfort in reminding myself that, just as you are with me now, you are with me always, every moment, as I parent a teenager. Teach me to look to you for all I need—wisdom, patience, self-control, love—a day at a time as I raise the teen you have entrusted to me. It's an overwhelming responsibility, but I know you don't leave me alone in it—and you never will. Keep me mindful of the resources your Holy Spirit and your written Word are for me, so that I will never be trying to do this crucial job in my own power or might. I pray in Jesus' name. Amen.

Eleven

Dealing with Specific Teenage Issues

Parenting Principles

- Parents need to provide principles to help teenagers make good decisions in areas like music, clothing, sex, and substances.
- During these years, parents need to remember to use grace, truth, and time and to be flexible.
- Parents need to have their own limits and the proper stance toward pleasure to develop delay of gratification in their teens.

We are strong believers in principles, because principles tell you how to handle almost any situation. So, we usually do not talk about "how to handle" specifics. But some specific situations are very common in dealing with teens.

Music (page 195)

- What value is there in letting your teenagers have their own musical choices in terms of style, beat, kind, and decibel level?

- What kind of limits are essential? Consider what the lyrics say. What limits does the Golden Rule suggest? Consider when the stereo is on and how loud the volume is.

- What kind of homework does a parent have to do before limiting a teen's music?

- What consequences can help you enforce the limits you set?

Hair, Clothes, Earrings, Appearance (page 195)

- What are some appropriate limits in this category—and why are they appropriate?

- Again, what homework does a parent have to do before limiting a young person's dress?

- When limits need to be set and consequences enforced, how will you offer both grace and truth? How will you show your empathy as you say no?

Curfew (page 196)

- Describe how freedom within limits can work when it comes to setting a curfew.

• What is your current policy on curfew and why? What are you doing to enforce it?

• What does it mean that "the limit was made for your child, not your child for the limit"? Explain, using a hypothetical or real-life situation.

Spirituality (page 196)

 • "Up to the late teen years, we would suggest doing everything possible to get them to attend church and Sunday school. But do give them a choice." Consider your current policy on church attendance in light of this statement. What is your current policy? How do you enforce it? And how are your teenagers responding? What changes might be in order?

• Comment on the value of setting this limit for a young adult: "Our family reserves this time for God. You don't have to go to church if you don't want to, but you can't do anything else either." Hint: This approach may keep you from turning religion into a control issue.

• What are you doing now to live out your spiritual values of love, faithfulness, honesty, compassion, forgiveness, stewardship of talents and life, and hope?

Sex and Substances (page 197)

Give your teenagers good education about sex, alcohol, and marijuana (and harder drugs).

- *Sex:* Teenagers need models and reality education.

  — What are you doing to be positive about sex and serious about the limits? What realities have you talked about with your teen as you've set limits?

- What are you doing to be sure to avoid sending messages about guilt and shame?

  — If your teenager is sexually active, what will you do to find out why? See the discussion on page 198 for some possible reasons.

- *Substances (tobacco, alcohol, marijuana, and harder stuff):* Again, teenagers need models and reality education.

  — What realities have you talked about with your teen as you've set forth limits?

  — What kind of modeling are you doing at home?

  — If your teenager is using illegal substances, what steps will you take to deal with this serious problem?

Studies (page 199)

By and large, teenagers should be managing their own study time. You manage the grades. Figure out what is reasonable to expect from each of your teens and then expect it. Regard deviations from your expectations as a sign that they are not managing their school life by themselves, and give them consequences.

 • What do you expect from your teenagers in the way of academics, grades, and school involvement?

• What can falling grades be a sign of? Find out the "why" before you give the discipline.

 • What kinds of consequences do you use to enforce your standards?

In all of these areas—music, appearance, curfew, spirituality, sex and substances, and studies—the message is simple and the ingredients are clear. The message is "some things are dangerous, so stay away from them; some things are not wise, so do not do them; some things are not moral, so avoid them; and you are in charge until you prove you cannot be."

The ingredients of parenting are grace (show your teenagers that you are for them); truth (show your teenagers what is right and enforce it with correction, limits, and reality consequences); time (teenagers are learning to guard and manage themselves: it is a process); and flexibility (in this dance, both you and your teenager are changing your roles).

Living with and Accepting Imperfection in Themselves and Others (page 200)

Teens have totally unrealistic standards for themselves and sometimes for others. They go up and down with their own failures and successes. Help them to accept themselves as they are with a goal of always getting better.

- What do you remember of this roller-coaster ride? Write down some thoughts. They may help you empathize with your teenager.

- The best defense against imperfection is love. To the degree that your teenagers feel loved, they will be able to accept their imperfections. Do not devalue their feelings, but empathize and accept them. Give your teenagers lots of positive feedback on their strengths and talents.

  — As your teens test the limits, fail, and sin, what will you do and say to make sure that you are facing the issues with grace? Not shaming or condemning is the first step.

  — What will you do to stay calm and give empathy and understanding even when your teenagers are hating you? Don't allow them to verbally attack you, but what will you do to show that you accept their feelings?

  — What does the statement "You don't have to become a teenager to deal with one!" mean to you?

Empathize with your teenagers' heartache and sadness, sexual frustrations, and "less than holy attitudes," and then contain and structure their anger. Above all, let them know that forgiveness is always available, no matter what they do (Ephesians 4:32).

Frustration Tolerance and Delay of Gratification (page 201)

Delay of gratification comes from a parent having limits and the proper stance toward pleasure. Teach young people that pleasure is good, but for pleasure that lasts, we have to work first.

- How did you learn delay of gratification as you were growing up? What lesson(s), if any, do you clearly remember?

- To teach your teenagers to learn to wait, make sure that you limit what is limitable so they will limit what is more intangible. For example, if you want them to wait for sex, which you cannot control, teach them to wait for a new piece of sports equipment until they earn half the money. What is important is that young people learn to delay gratification until they do their part.

  — What experience in delayed gratification has your teenager had? What, for instance, have good grades earned her?

  — What current opportunity to teach delayed gratification do you have? Does your teenager want to have a car of his own or use of your car? What will you require of him before he has a car or drives yours?

  — What will you say in response to your teenager's protests ("That's not fair. Bill is getting one!")?

Teenagers need to learn to delay gratification until they do their part. Encourage and help them along the way without enabling them by bailing them out and making life seem easier than it really is. Help them learn to work first and play later. It will serve them for a lifetime.

Social Group Demands and Interpersonal Skills (page 202)

Teens should be involved in large group activities as well as dating and opposite-sex relationships. Healthy teens also usually have a clan that they run around with.

- What evidence do you see that your teenager is socializing in these normal, healthy ways?

- What do you do to make your home a friendly place where your teenagers— and their friends—want to hang out? Is there a Ping-Pong table in the garage, Coke in the refrigerator, and a bag of chips always in the pantry?

- If your teenager seems to be going through a difficult time socially, see what you can do to help. If something is absent, ask about it. Maybe they don't feel likable, so they do not venture out. They may need some help or counseling. Maybe they have had a heartbreak they're not telling you about.

  — If your teenagers are not talking to you, address that issue first.

  — If (or when) communication is good, try to help them get past the social hurdle that they are facing. If, for instance, you see a character pattern that is costing your teenager friendships, let them know.

Talents, Abilities, and Interests (page 203)

Consider the following points about talents, abilities, and interests that you can focus on to help your teen develop.

- Which of these guidelines did your parents follow when you were growing up? How did you benefit? Be specific.

  1. Make sure your teenagers' interests are theirs, not yours.

  2. Support them in what they do choose.

  3. Require your teens to stick with extracurricular activities, especially if you pay.

  4. Expose them to a lot of choices, and to an extent, help in creating opportunities.

  5. Share activities and skills with your teenagers.

 • Which of these guidelines have you been following either instinctively or consciously? Give evidence supporting your answers.

  1. Make sure your teenagers' interests are theirs, not yours.

  2. Support them in what they do choose.

3. Require your teens to stick with extracurricular activities, especially if you pay.

4. Expose them to a lot of choices, and to an extent, help in creating opportunities.

5. Share activities and skills with your teenagers.

- Which of these five pieces of parental advice do you need to follow more closely? Be specific about the changes in your parenting they suggest.

The Result (page 204)

If you do all that these two chapters outline, then your adolescents will be new people at the end of the process. You will have friends for life—friends of whom you can be proud and whom you can watch unfold as God directs their steps into the future. You will have given your teenagers roots and wings. You will have given them what they need to go out into the world on their own: character.

- If you and your parents are friends, to what do you attribute that wonderful outcome? Learn from your own experience.

- If you and your parents aren't friends, what interfered along the way? Again, learn from your own experience.

If you give your teenagers the process of freedom, discipline, love, support, and forgiveness to help them become their own people, that is something to be proud of as you let go and retire from your job as parent.

Hands-on Exercise

If You Do One Thing Besides Pray . . .

Review the topics covered in this chapter. List the areas where you need to do some homework. What specific concerns do you have for your teenager? Why? And what are you going to do about those concerns?

Also, if you haven't already, talk to a parent of a teenager or adult child who seems to be on the right track. Let the focus of your conversation be "What, if anything, can I be doing now to smooth the road of adolescence for my teenager, for myself, and for our relationship?" Perhaps someone else's Monday-morning quarterbacking will give you some insight and tips.

Folded-Hands Exercise

"My help comes from the LORD . . ."

—PSALM 121:2

"Give teenagers the process of freedom, discipline, love, support, and forgiveness to help them become their own people." On paper that sounds simple enough, but, Lord, this phase of parenting is anything but easy! There's a dizzying array of issues to be aware of and to be ready to address—music, hair, clothes, appearance, curfew, spirituality, sex and substances, studies. Help me offer both grace and truth as I address these matters. Help me offer love and empathy as my teens continue to deal with their own imperfections and learn to tolerate frustration and delay gratification. Show me how to help my teenagers be good stewards of the talents, abilities, and interests you have given them. Thank you that you are with me as I tackle this challenging phase of parenting. May I rely on your constant presence with me and your available supply of wisdom and strength as I face each day's challenges. I pray in Jesus' name. Amen.

Part Four

———

Dealing with Special Circumstances

—— Twelve ——

Understanding Temperaments

┌─ Parenting Principles ──────────────────────────────┐

- Temperament is an inborn style of relating to the world, and that style is different in different kids.
- Character is the ability to function in life. It is more important than temperament.
- Temperament should not excuse improper behavior; it can be modified with experience.

└───┘

Temperament has to do with certain categories of inborn traits that cause people to respond differently to life. This may include tendencies toward introversion or extroversion and toward activity or passivity, for example. Many parents wonder about how to deal with temperaments. The teenage years can also be quite confusing because adolescent moods and styles change drastically, seemingly out of the blue.

Temperament Is Not Character (page 207)

Temperament is a style of relating to the world: individual differences, from energy level to academic interests, make up your teenager's unique soul. Character, however, is not a style: character is a set of abilities necessary to function in the world. Character is neither an option nor an alternative. It is a requirement for survival. Character comes first and style second.

- If you have brothers and sisters, what different temperaments are represented among you? Is one of you outgoing and one more reserved? Is one more active and another more passive? How, if at all, did your parents compensate for that—or how could they have done so?

- You need to help your teenagers mature in all of the character traits we've written about in this book. But take their individuality into consideration as you do.

  — Make this statement more personal. What, for instance, does your sensitive teen need in the way of correction? your high-energy teen?

 — Describe your teenager's temperament. How do you—or could you— adjust your parenting to your teen's temperament while teaching the essentials of character?

Whatever your teenager's temperament, the task of learning responsibility is the same. All teenagers, whatever their style, need to take ownership of their lives.

- One of the difficulties of parenting is that your teenager needs your help in all areas of character, but you most likely won't excel in all. Your ability in each area is not the same.

  — In which of the following areas do you feel strong and able to parent? Put a star next to those.

  Attachment

  Responsibility

  Reality

  Competence

Morality

Worship and Spiritual Life

— Which of these six aspects of character are areas that you need to or would like to strengthen? What will you do toward that end?

We can't overemphasize the importance of finding help from others for your weak areas. Your parenting experiences will expose these weaknesses. When that happens, turn to God, his resources, and his people for relationship, healing, and growth.

How to Tell the Difference (page 209)

It is sometimes difficult to tell if a problem is temperament-influenced or character-based, because the outworking of each is similar. You may notice, for example, that your fourteen-year-old son is more energetic and active than his buddies. He may have a hard time sitting still, paying attention in school, and keeping himself focused on tasks. Some of this behavior may be due to his more active temperament. He is just wired to be more active, rather than calm and docile. But some of this behavior may also be due to a lack of structure and the absence of consequences that can help him settle down. No one knows what percentage is one or the other.

The important thing is to provide enough boundaries in your teenagers' experience for them to be able to be the self-controlled people God intended, not adults who have learned to excuse their inappropriate behavior by saying, "That's just the way I am."

Again, it's sometimes difficult to tell if a problem is temperament- or character-based. An expert (such as a teacher or psychologist) can be helpful, but we want to point out a basic difference in temperament-influenced behavior and character-based issues: When character issues are resolved, the remaining temperament issues don't tend to be a major problem.

- Read that statement again: When character issues are resolved, the remaining temperament issues don't tend to be a major problem. When, if ever, have you seen the truth of this statement in real life? (Consider the example given above.) More specifically, when have you seen the resolution of a character issue bring a temperament more into the range of "normal" or acceptable?

- If you see in your teenager a tendency that concerns you, a good rule of thumb is to investigate it first as a character issue.

  — Review the six questions listed on pages 209–10 of the text and those listed below.

    Is your teenager's behavior a way to seek attachment and relationship?

    Does it show a lack of personal boundaries and responsibility?

    Is your teenager trying to cover up weakness and vulnerability by being aggressive?

    Could your teenager's behavior be a response to an inner perfectionism?

  — Why does a yes answer to any of these questions suggest a character issue—a matter of attachment, responsibility, reality, competence, morality, or worship and spiritual life—rather than a temperament issue?

  — If you can answer yes to any of the questions, what could you do to address the character problem you have just identified in your teenager? Think about what you have been learning in the text and this workbook.

Most of the time a behavioral problem is a matter of character, especially with regard to disruptive problems. Differences in temperaments don't tend to be as extreme.

So What? (page 210)

Now let's imagine some teenagers who are struggling with an issue that is 0 percent character and 100 percent temperament. If that's the case, even though their temperament is not their fault, they are increasingly responsible for dealing with it as they grow up. In life we deal not only with problems we have caused, but also with problems not caused by us. Thus, we need to solve problems, not establish blame.

- What aspects of your temperament have you struggled to become responsible for rather than simply falling back on "I can't help it. That's just how I am"? What has helped you to be victorious in this struggle that might help your teenager do the same?

- When do parents deal with temperament as a problem, not a "way of being"? Here is the rule: Deal with temperament when it inhibits growth in attachment, responsibility or ownership, reality, competence, morality, or worship and spiritual life, the six aspects of character growth.

  — Where, if at all, has your teen's temperament been inhibiting growth in one of the six areas of character growth we have been considering? Your teenager, for example, may by nature be more introverted than others. So she may still need you to help her adapt her temperament to reality and not demand the reverse. In other words, your teen's tendency to be quiet and by herself needs to change because reality won't. She can't live life without interacting with other people.

  — Review the chapter in the text that addresses the particular aspect of character growth you just identified as a problem area. What will you do to help your teen?

— How will relationship with you help your teenager deal with this aspect of character growth? Remember that relationship is key!

Styles and temperaments can be modified with experience. Research has shown that environment has a powerful effect even on inborn traits. This is a testimony to the redemptive work of God: our traits don't determine our lives.

The Strong-Willed Child (page 211)

Some parents avoid confronting the determination of strong-willed kids to have life their own way. These parents don't want to squelch their will or discourage them from being decisive. At the same time, they are concerned about helping the kids mind them and learn obedience.

• Is your teenager strong-willed? Give some specific evidence supporting why you answered the question the way you did.

• In what ways can the following parental tools help soften that strong will? Be specific.

— Love

— Empathy

— Correction

— Experience

— Consequences

We have seen many examples where people have been able to make significant changes in their kids' lives using these principles.

The strong-willed child's power should end where the family's peace of mind begins. In other words, encourage your teen's assertiveness, but do not allow it to disrupt the family's functioning.

Hands-on Exercise

If You Do One Thing Besides Pray . . .

Spend some time working specifically on a weak area in your own character so that you can be more effective in helping your teenager develop in that area. Develop a plan of action and then do it.

Folded-Hands Exercise

"My help comes from the LORD . . ."

—PSALM 121:2

Almighty God, you knit together my teenager. You know my teenager well. You created that unique soul, temperament, personality, and you gave me the privilege of being a parent to that teen. Lord, sometimes as a parent I'm at a loss about whether I'm dealing with a character problem or a temperament problem. Thank you for giving wisdom when we ask—I'm asking! Thank you for blessing us with creativity when we need to solve problems—I'm in need! And thank you for being strong when I am weak—and I'm weak in certain aspects of character, but I still need my kids to learn those.

Please, Lord, as I parent my teenagers, may I know your presence with me in a very tangible, real way so that I may have insight into my kids (is the situation a matter of temperament or character?) and wisdom about how to resolve that issue and raise them to please and honor you. Thank you that you redeem my mistakes and my teenagers' weaknesses, temperament as well as character flaws. I pray in Jesus' name. Amen.

——— Thirteen ———

Parenting on Your Own

Even if you're married, be sure to work through the "When to Get Help" section that begins on page 216. It's important for all parents to know when they are dealing with a parenting problem that is beyond their resources.

┌─ Parenting Principles ─────────────

- Single parenting has its own set of challenges as you make sure that your teenager gets the resources that two parents would normally provide.
- Parents (single or otherwise) need to first evaluate the severity of their children's problems and then decide how to approach those problems.
- God is especially accessible to assist the child of the single parent (Psalm 68:5).

The other material in this workbook certainly applies to you, but we wanted to include a special section that speaks to the particular challenges you face as a single parent. Parenting on your own is very difficult and brings its own set of problems. And now your teenager needs you at this critical developmental juncture. So, if you are a single parent, our hearts go out to you as you deal with both personal and parenting losses. Know, however, that God understands your struggle and that he is close to the brokenhearted (Psalm 34:8).

The Conditions (page 213)

To help you parent your teenagers, we are going to look at some of the main conditions that a two-parent household is able to deal with in order to help you understand what your teen needs. Then, for each condition, we will provide suggestions on how you, as a single parent, can help your teen in these areas.

• ***Children—of any age—ideally need two parents to meet their varied needs.***

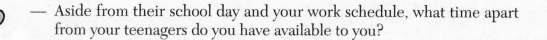 — What do you see as your strengths and your weaknesses? Be sure to specifically address the six aspects of character we've been considering.

    — What healthy relationships are you involved in—or could you become involved in? Among these people, whom can you ask to help you in the areas where you are weak?

• ***Children are demanding.***

    — Aside from their school day and your work schedule, what time apart from your teenagers do you have available to you?

    — What friends and family members can assist you so that you come back to your teenagers refreshed and looking forward to connecting with them?

• ***Parenting is basically relationship.***

    — What models of healthy relationship do you or could you make available to your teenager?

— What are you doing to keep at bay the enemies of isolation and self-sufficiency?

— What regular times do you set aside to invest in relationship for yourself?

- ***Two parents help children enter the world of other people.***

— Your teenagers need to learn to invest in and trust other people. Why is this important? And who in your teenagers' world can help them learn these important skills? Church singles groups, Bible studies, and home support groups can be good sources of safe friendships, as well as being involved with loving, stable married friends.

— Single moms need to find stable, healthy men whom they aren't dating to help kids enter the world of other people. Who in your life falls into that category—or where might you get to know such a person?

- ***Two parents help kids move out of self-centeredness.***

— Whom do your teenagers see you loving besides them? Why is this important for your teens?

— What adults besides you is your teen involved with? Though adolescents are highly invested in their peer group, they also need adult interaction.

- ***Parents also provide a check and balance on each other.***

— We all have our blind spots. Whom do you let close enough to see your blind spots and help you work on your parenting faults?

— What good support groups for single parents are available to you? Look into local church and community groups.

If you are single through divorce, keep in mind that, if you and your ex are good coparents, you can complete many of the tasks just outlined by working together. Blessed are the children whose parents sacrifice their conflicts to help them mature.

A Word About Dating (page 215)

- Review the discussion of dating. What words of caution speak to you most powerfully? What changes, if any, do you need to make in your dating life or in your perspective on dating and its purpose?

- Summarize in your own words the importance of not putting your teenager's needs into your date's hands.

Enjoy your dating life. Don't hide from your teenager the fact that you date. But remember that your date isn't your teen's parent and won't be until and unless you marry. Keep the two processes distinct.

When to Get Help (page 216)

How do you know when you are dealing with a parenting problem that is beyond your resources? So many problems have a range of severity, and God has equipped parents to solve most problems. However, sometimes you need to contact a child therapist or specialist. Here are some guidelines to follow.

- ***Pray:*** As a parent, you have some insight into how much your heavenly Father wants to help you.

  — What encouragement do you find in the truths of Proverbs 2:6 and James 1:5?

  — What current parenting struggles, if any, do you want to bring before the Lord? Let him know that you are dependent on him and that you need his help.

- ***Stay or get connected to your teenager:*** Relationship with your teens can help you learn information you need in order to decide how to solve problems.

  — In what context is your teenager most likely to talk about what's going on, about thoughts and feelings, hopes and fears? Make a date, pray about the time in advance, and then, when you're together, listen for what your teen is—and is not—saying.

— What other adults have a close or relatively close relationship with your teenager? What insight does one or two of those people have into the issue you are praying about?

- ***Always make sure your teenager is in ongoing medical care:*** Sometimes behavior problems are physiological in nature.

    — When was your teen's last doctor's appointment or checkup?

    — What is the overall condition of your teenager's health? What kind of diet and sleep schedule is she keeping? Is she drinking a lot of coffee or caffeinated soda pop? What has your doctor said about the problem you are concerned and praying about? Talk to your doctor if you haven't already.

- ***Stay in a healthy, child-wise community:*** Being around a healthy church with a good youth ministry is extremely valuable to a single parent.

    — What do your teen's youth group leaders say about his attitude, behaviors, and friendships? Does the youth pastor have any insight or ideas about how you can help your teenager with the issue you're concerned about?

    — If you're not involved in a church, what research will you do this week to find out which local churches are healthy and have a strong youth program for your teenager?

- **_Deal with your desire to not be at fault:_** A great hindrance to finding out your teenager's problem can be your own fear of being found to be lacking in your parenting. Remember that all parents are lacking in some way and that God heals the sick, not the well (Matthew 9:12–13).

  — What lies behind your wishes to be a perfect parent? Where can you go to find healthy relationships with people who accept you, warts and all? This acceptance can help you accept yourself.

  — Take some time—alone with the Lord or with a trusted friend or family member as well—to look in the mirror and honestly consider whether your parenting style is part of your teenager's problem. Your teen may even offer some insight about, for instance, his falling grades (ask the question "Can you think of any way I make it hard for you to study?"), and your friends might help you see how you're enabling your teen's bad grades. If you see that your parenting is part of the problem, then decide what you will do to change your style in order to help your teenager.

- **_Investigate the problem as a character issue:_** Explore whether or not your teenager's struggle has to do with problems with relationship, responsibility, reality, competence, talents, spiritual issues, or letting go. For example, if your teen is struggling with a chronically rebellious attitude, you may be dealing with a disobedience problem, he may be struggling in some relationship, or he may need more or less structure.

  — Is there a teacher, coach, youth group leader, Sunday school teacher, or other significant person who can help you with the diagnosis?

— Once the character issue has been identified (if that does indeed seem to be the root of your teen's problem), determine how you will deal with that issue and what you will consider signs of improvement in your teen's behavior.

- **Give "character work" time to take effect:** If you are dealing with a character issue, allow the process some time.

  — What does your teenager need to unlearn? How long has that behavior been part of her repertoire?

  — Who among the adults in your teenager's life can join you in your effort? What might a teacher, coach, or youth worker do to help this "character work" happen?

- **Get help when all the above doesn't work over time:** Even with the right ingredients—grace, truth, and time—some emotional and behavioral problems go beyond normal parenting resources. Fighting, academic failure, isolation, and low motivation levels that don't get better over time are signs that you need to get more help. Find a specialist.

  — What resources are available to you?

  — Whom will you consult for referrals?

- **Look for red flags that mean "get help":** Some serious issues won't improve and may worsen until an expert intervenes. Get help quickly if you see any of the symptoms listed on pages 218–19 in the text.

  — What symptoms, if any, do you see in your teenager?

  — What promises from Scripture can you cling to if you see some of these red flags in your teen?

Fortunately, with the right interventions, many of these issues can be resolved. Some may take much time, energy, and resources. Stay connected to your own support system and, whatever you do, stay as involved as possible with your teenager. Many teens with serious problems go on to establish good, productive lives because they had parents who got help in time and assisted them in working through it.

Single parenting requires much of a mom or dad. However, God is right there with appropriate resources to help you shore up the areas in which you are lacking skills, knowledge, or energy. God bless you as, with his guidance, you raise a great kid.

Hands-on Exercise

If You Do One Thing Besides Pray . . .

Take some time this week to evaluate the support system you currently have for yourself. Who can be (or perhaps already is) a partner in parenting? Who offers your teenager a good role model and the chance to enter the world of relationships with other people besides you? What holes do you see in your support system? What will you do to strengthen the good ties you have to people? What will you do to fill in any gaps you have identified? Prayer for the Lord's guidance and provision is always a good first step.

Folded-Hands Exercise

"My help comes from the LORD . . ."

—PSALM 121:2

Father God, I find great hope in the fact that you are close to the brokenhearted and that your strength is made perfect in my human weakness. And, Lord, nothing like parenting alone has made me so aware of my weaknesses and therefore of my need for you. So I come before you, Lord, thankful that you love my teenager even more than I do, that you give wisdom when I ask, and that you are a Redeemer God who can help me parent my teenager despite this less-than-ideal situation and my very human weaknesses. Lord, I need you—and I believe you will help me each step of the way. Help my unbelief. I pray in Jesus' name. Amen.

Conclusion
When in Doubt, Connect

┌ Parenting Principles ──────────────────

- Your child is also God's child—and he will not forsake his own.
- Parenting cannot be done in a vacuum: you need supportive relationships.
- When you don't know how to deal with a problem with your teenager, your first move is to connect with him or her.

Raising great kids is a goal that is both overwhelming and frightening for many parents. The responsibility of having someone's life in your hands, knowing your own failings, can make anyone anxious and unsure. In addition, the amount of material we've included in this book can be daunting. You may wonder if you can do all the work on character development we have presented. We address these concerns in these final pages.

The Divine View (page 221)

You need to understand your parenting from God's point of view.

- Remember that God chose you to be your teen's parent. God chose you to be his "hands and feet" in dispensing his grace and truth to your adolescent. He is helping, guiding, and supporting you, and he is not surprised by the twists and turns of the process. The parenting job is a large one, but not too large for you and God. He trusts you with the teenager he has given you, and he has equipped you for the task.

— What new idea, if any, did you find in this paragraph?

— What particular phrases do you find especially comforting and encouraging?

- Remember, too, that your child is also God's child, and he will not forsake his own (Deuteronomy 31:6, 8). God forbid that you would ever shirk your duties to your teenagers. But even if you did, God would not leave them unattended: "Though my father and mother forsake me, the LORD will receive me" (Psalm 27:10).

    — What evidence of God's great faithfulness did you experience when you were a teenager?

    — What specific evidence of God's faithfulness to your own teens have you seen?

When God calls, he enables. Nowhere will that truth be more encouraging than in your parenting.

Parents Need Support (page 222)

The Lord will indeed support your parenting efforts, but you also need the help and support of others. You can't parent well in a vacuum.

- You don't have everything your teenager needs, and you need to get what you don't possess from warm, honest people. You need to be in regular, vulnerable contact with people who are helping you grow not only as a parent but also personally and spiritually as an individual.

    — What does your teenager need that you aren't able to provide? Who is helping you to fill that gap?

— Who in your life helps you grow as a parent? Who is helping you grow personally and spiritually? If your list is short or nonexistent, what will you do to get connected with warm, honest people? Be specific—and take the first step before the month is out. (The tips in the next question may help. So might our book *Safe People*. It describes how to look for and evaluate people and groups that are spiritually and emotionally good for you. Chapter 11, "Where Are the Safe People?," not only has information on good people but also a section on evaluating good churches.)

• Being a parent doesn't automatically mean you are in community. Take steps to find what resources are in your area for help with both parenting and personal/spiritual growth. Many churches now have parenting classes and fellowship groups for parents. Or you might organize friends, neighbors, or other parents of teens to trade parenting problems and tips, and perhaps even to pray. If these groups are to be helpful, they need to be safe places where people can be open, centered on healthy parenting, and meeting regularly.

 — What community, if any, does being a parent of a teenager make you a part of?

 — What support do local organizations, community programs, and churches offer you? What programs and support are available for you and your teen?

Very few children have the benefit of being raised by their extended families. So, as parents, we need to supplement our efforts with the love and support of people who aren't related to us by blood.

Use the Structure (page 223)

Kids of all ages can cause a lot of chaos in life, and you need to know where the parenting process is now and where it is going. So we hope you will use this book as a road map pointing you to the six areas in which your teenager needs to be growing.

- Familiarize yourself with the six character traits and address them.

    — In what ways have you already noticed these six touchstones of parenting organizing and focusing your parenting efforts? Be specific.

    — In what ways have you and your spouse enjoyed a stronger partnership since you started thinking together about these six aspects of character development?

    — What have you realized about your teenagers since opening *Raising Great Kids*? What specific steps toward facilitating their character growth have you taken? What growth have you seen?

Again, let this book be a road map that gives you an idea of where you need to go as a parent so that your teenager is not merely a good kid, but a great kid, a kid of solid and godly character.

Normalize Failure (page 223)

You want to parent the right way, and you don't want your failures to hurt your children. The sad reality is that you have failed in the past and you will fail in the future. You can't love, provide structure for, and teach your teenagers perfectly every time. And your failures do affect your children.

- It is much better for a teenager to have parents who admit failure, ask for forgiveness, and change as they learn from their errors. Be a parent who is not afraid of failure, but sees it as a way to grow. Be less afraid of mistakes and more afraid of denying them.

  — How did your own parents deal with their mistakes? What did their denial or openness teach you about failure?

  — What do you want your teenager to understand about failure? What are you doing to teach that?

The bad news is that you will make mistakes as you parent. The good news is that kids are resilient and they can recover and flourish under imperfect parents.

When in Doubt, Connect (page 224)

Parenting is unpredictable because kids are unpredictable. You are dealing with human beings who are complex, impulsive, contradictory, wanting total freedom, and always in transition.

- When you don't know what to do, what do you do? This is a question all parents face.

  — When have you been at the limits of your understanding and parenting abilities? What factors contributed to that feeling—pressure at work, the demands of daily living, your health? Be specific.

  — "When in doubt, connect." If you followed that bit of advice intuitively, what were the results? Connection never hurts, often helps, and sometimes is the entire solution to the problem.

- When your teenager is frustrating, provocative, or hurtful, connection may not be the first thing you think of. But connection is essential to helping your teen be rooted and grounded in love (Ephesians 3:17).

  — What behavior do you tend to fall into when your teen is being frustrating, provocative, or hurtful? See a list of possibilities on pages 224–25.

  — Explain in your own words why relationship is the most important of all the character aspects discussed in this book. If ideas don't come easily, review the discussion of connection on pages 224–26 of the text's conclusion.

  — When you encounter an unsolvable problem, take steps to move toward your teenagers in a way that they can experience that you are with and for them and know that you want to understand their internal world. What kinds of steps could you take that would be appropriate and meaningful for your teen? The chart (page 226 in the text) gives two examples.

  — Of course, we are not saying to only connect when there are problems. (That creates a problem all its own!) What are you doing to give your teenager sustained and constant love?

Sometimes connection solves the problem, but sometimes it is only the first of many, many steps toward solving it. So teach your teenager by word and deed that being in relationship is very important. Through good times and bad, make attachment the norm of your teenager's existence. And may you know God's blessing as you continue to seek what is best for your teenager.

Hands-on Exercise

If You Do One Thing Besides Pray . . .

Choose three or four verses from Scripture that are especially encouraging to you as a parent. (Several are referred to in this chapter, and maybe you've noticed others throughout the text.) Memorize them so that they are hidden in your heart that you might not sin against your teenager or the Lord (Psalm 119:11). Let them be a source of encouragement when the demands of parenting a teenager temporarily outweigh the joys.

Folded-Hands Exercise

"My help comes from the LORD . . ."

—PSALM 121:2

Heavenly Father, you chose me to be my child's parent. My child is your child as well. You will never forsake my child (Psalm 27:10)—or me either (Deuteronomy 31:6). I can't parent well in a vacuum—and I know I shouldn't try to. I need to use this book as a road map, not a measuring stick that raps knuckles for insufficient progress. I need to admit failure to my kids, ask for forgiveness, and change as I learn from my errors. And when I am in doubt, I need to connect.

Lord, I want to take in these powerful truths as I spend time now in your presence, a presence that fills me with hope and reminds me that I am not alone in this wondrous privilege and daunting task of parenting. Enable me to be the parent you want me to be, willing to follow your example: you reconciled yourself to me first, knowing that I didn't have it in me to change until I was hooked up to you. Keep me from requiring that my child get it all together and only then make the connection. Teach me to love with a love that balances grace and truth in a way that guides my child on the path toward solid character and a life that will bring glory to you. I pray in Jesus' name. Amen.

For information about Dr. Henry Cloud and Dr. John Townsend's books, tapes, resources, and speaking engagements, contact:

Cloud-Townsend Resources
3176 Pullman Avenue, Suite 104
Costa Mesa, CA 92626
Telephone: 1–800–646–HOPE (4673)
Fax: 1–949–760–1839
Email: web@cloudtownsend.com
Website: www.cloudtownsend.com

Raising Great Kids

A Comprehensive Guide to Parenting with Grace and Truth
Foreword by Elisa Morgan
Dr. Henry Cloud & Dr. John Townsend

What Does It Take to Raise Great Kids?

If you've read any books on parenting, conflicting opinions may leave you feeling confused. Get tough! Show acceptance. Lay down the rules. Lighten up, already! There has to be a balance between control and permissiveness. And there is. Drs. Henry Cloud and John Townsend help you provide the care and acceptance that make grace real to your kids, and the firmness and discipline that give direction. At last, here is an effective middle ground for raising your children to handle life with maturity and wisdom.

Hardcover 0-310-22569-8
Softcover 0-310-23549-9
Audio 0-310-22572-8

Raising Great Kids Workbook for Parents of Preschoolers

A Comprehensive Guide to Parenting with Grace and Truth
Ages 0–5/Foreword by Elisa Morgan
Dr. Henry Cloud & Dr. John Townsend

Using principles described in *Raising Great Kids,* the *Raising Great Kids Workbook for Parents of Preschoolers* will guide you through those first, formative years in your child's life from infancy to age five. It's filled with sound biblical information and expert advice. But most important, it supplies tools you can begin using today, from thought-provoking questions and self-assessments to an abundance of practical applications. Each chapter begins by introducing three or four key parenting principles and ends with a hands-on exercise and prayer that crystallize the concepts dealt with in that chapter. The *Raising Great Kids Workbook for Parents of Preschoolers* will help you start sowing the seeds of character early in your child's life—for good fruit that lasts a lifetime.

Softcover 0-310-22571-X

Raising Great Kids Workbook for Parents of School-Age Children

A Comprehensive Guide to Parenting with Grace and Truth
Ages 6–12
Dr. Henry Cloud & Dr. John Townsend

The grade-school years from ages 6 to 12 are a time of learning more than reading, writing, and arithmetic. Your child is also developing the one thing above all others that will determine his or her success in life: character. The *Raising Great Kids Workbook for Parents of School-Age Children* helps you instill traits that are vital to your son or daughter's future well-being: connection, responsibility, reality, competence, morality, and worship/spiritual life.

Based on *Raising Great Kids,* this workbook is filled with self-tests, discussion material, exercises, and practical applications that can help you turn key concepts into a natural way of parenting. Here's help for teaching your child lessons no grade-school textbook covers.

Softcover 0-310-23452-2

Gold-Medallion Book by Dr. Henry Cloud & Dr. John Townsend
Voted 1993 Best Book of the Year

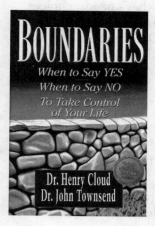

Boundaries

When to Say Yes, When to Say No to Take Control of Your Life
Dr. Henry Cloud & Dr. John Townsend

Is your life out of control?
Do people take advantage of you?
Do you have trouble saying no?
Are you disappointed with God because of unanswered prayers?

Having clear boundaries is essential to a healthy, balanced lifestyle. A boundary is a personal property line that marks those things for which we are responsible. In other words, boundaries define who we are and who we are not.

Boundaries impact all areas of our lives:
— Physical boundaries
— Mental boundaries
— Emotional boundaries
— Spiritual boundaries

Often Christians focus so much on being loving and unselfish that they forget their own limits and limitations. Drs. Henry Cloud and John Townsend offer biblically based answers to many tough questions, showing us how to set healthy boundaries with our parents, spouses, children, friends, coworkers, and even ourselves.

Pick up a copy today at your favorite local retailer!

Hardcover 0-310-58590-2

Also available:
Audio Pages 0-310-58598-8
Workbook 0-310-49481-8
Boundaries (Revised) Groupware 0-310-22362-8
Boundaries (Revised) Leader's Guide 0-310-2245-7
Boundaries (Revised) Participant's Guide 0-31022453-5

Boundaries in Marriage

Dr. Henry Cloud & Dr. John Townsend

It Takes Two Individuals to Become One Flesh

Only when you and your mate know and respect each other's needs, choices, and freedom can you give yourselves freely and lovingly to one another. *Boundaries in Marriage* gives you the tools you need. Drs. Henry Cloud and John Townsend, counselors and authors of the award-winning best-seller *Boundaries,* share with you:

— Why boundaries are vital for a thriving, productive marriage
— How values form the structure and architecture of marriage
— How to protect your marriage from intruders, whether other people or personal idols
— Why each partner needs to establish personal boundaries and how to go about it
— How to work with a spouse who understands and values boundaries—and how to work with one who doesn't

This book helps you understand the friction points—even the serious hurts in your marriage—and enables you to move beyond them to mutual care, respect, affirmation, and intimacy.

Hardcover 0-310-22151-X

Also available:
Audio Pages 0-310-22549-3
Unabridged Audio Pages 0-310-23849-8
Workbook 0-310-22875-1

Boundaries with Kids
When to Say Yes, When to Say No to Help Your Children Gain Control of Their Lives

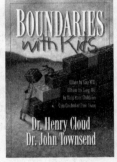

Want to Paint a Happy Future for Your Children? Start Drawing the Line Today.

You want your kids to grow up into healthy adults and take responsibility for their behavior, their values, and their lives. But maybe you've discovered that simply telling them to "do the right thing" isn't enough. From toddler tantrums to teenage temptations, you have to help them take ownership of their behavior, feelings, and attitudes. But how?

Establish healthy boundaries. Boundaries are the bedrock of good relationships, maturity, safety, and growth for your children and for you. In *Boundaries with Kids,* Drs. Henry Cloud and John Townsend show you how to bring control to an out-of-control family life. How to set limits and still be a loving parent. How to define legitimate boundaries for your family. And above all, how to instill in your children the kind of godly character that is the foundation for healthy, productive adult living.

Hardcover 0-310-20035-0

Also available:
Audio Pages 0-310-20456-9
Workbook 0-310-22349-0

Other Books by Dr. Henry Cloud

Changes That Heal

How to Understand Your Past to Ensure a Healthier Future

Softcover 0-310-60631-4

Also Available:
Mass Market 0-310-21463-7
Audio Pages 0-310-20567-0
Workbook 0-310-60633-0

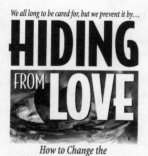

Hiding from Love

How to Change the Withdrawal Patterns That Isolate and Imprison You

Softcover 0-310-20107-1

We want to hear from you. Please send your comments about this book to us in care of the address below. Thank you.

ZondervanPublishingHouse
Grand Rapids, Michigan

A Division of HarperCollins*Publishers*